UNDO
ORDINARY

KEYS TO UNLOCKING
YOUR PURPOSE

RICO MILLER

Copyright

ISBN 978-0-578-59354-8

Printed in the United States of America
Cover Design & Layout by: Kingdom Branding

Dedication

I dedicate this book to the following people:

My grandmothers Florine Scandrett and Loverta Miller. I know you are smiling down on me while wearing your heavenly crowns. I love you both with all my heart. I also dedicate this book to my friend and brother, the late Jason Moore, who was one of my biggest supporters. I love you, my brother!

Acknowledgments

To My Heavenly Father and Lord. It is because of your extraordinary love that I had a fighting chance. I am nothing without you, but everything with you. Thank you for trusting me with this assignment. Thank you for creating a pathway to the vision you had called for my life. I am humbled by the love you have for me. I am eternally grateful. I will forever spend my life helping others come into the realization of your mercy and grace over them.

To my amazing parents, George and Sandra Miller. I am who I am today because of you. Your sacrifices and encouragement allowed me to believe that I could accomplish anything if I put my mind to it. Through Christ, all things are possible.

To my siblings: Ashley, Sergio. Thank you for your continual support. I love you dearly.

To my nieces, MaKayla, Sydney and a host of other cousins and family members. Thank you for your unconditional love and support.

To my wonderful church family, Pastor Aaron Robinson, and the entire Mount Welcome Missionary Baptist Church. Thank you for your support.

To Rotimi Kehinde and the team at Kingdom Branding, Ayana McDonald, Dawn Moore, and the entire Rico Miller Ministries Team. Thank you for your incredible contributions to this project.

Contents

Preface

After several years of ministry, I have arrived at the conclusion that ministry can be quite draining. It has the propensity to leave you mentally exhausted. In a lot of ways, doing the work of ministry can cause you to become weary in well-doing. Ministry workers tend to deal with a long list of things, including loneliness, feelings of powerlessness, and fatigue. I know fatigue quite well myself, so much that I have, oftentimes, found myself on a journey of seeking options or ways to replenish the vigor, the zest, and zeal, that I had when I entered ministry 10 years ago. I found myself doing things that I felt ministers ordinarily do in practice or routine. I began to live someone else's norm but not my own. I began to think there was something more than this mundane draining, day in and day out scenario. I wanted more out of my life and ministry. I wanted more than I was experiencing. Have you ever been there before? Have you looked for the feelings that existed when you first answered the call to ministry, accepted the job, got married or experienced other events you consider important to you?

In the absence of zeal, and all the wonderful feelings that consumed me when I first started, many questions came to mind.

Am I doing this the right way?
Is this everything I thought it would be?
Is this really what God has called me to?

Did I say yes too soon?
Do I truly have what it takes?

It frequently felt as though I had more questions than there were answers. There were even times when I felt as though the questions I had were considered dumb. As a kid, I remember asking my grandmothers, who were both true fountains of wisdom, tons of questions. My grandmothers were strong, resilient, virtuous women. One thing I appreciated about them is how they never made me feel like a burden when I would come and load them down with questions. Instead, they offered a safe place for me to express myself, and ultimately, be challenged in a much-needed way. I remember, one day, my grandmother said I had a lot of questions and this was a good thing. She assured me that the smartest people are not the ones with all the right answers, but those who have the right questions.

While I haven't quite figured everything out and I don't consider to know it all, I have learned the power of asking questions. Asking questions is a step in the right direction; it's part of the recipe for momentum and motion. If your life has lacked movement for some time, ask yourself these questions. When is the last time you asked a question? When was the last time you asked, "Why am I here?" "Am I living the life I envisioned for myself?" "Am I asking the right questions and leaving my heart open to feedback? "

At times, we feel motionless, yet, we are full of emotion.

Oftentimes, when we feel burdened, we can't quite find the words to express it because life has left us speechless. During these moments, I am reminded of a story that most of us have heard several times. A crippled man sits among people that seem to be doing quite well in comparison to his subpar ordinary life. Almost everyone in this city, including this man, has some type of illness. One of the only differences between this man and those around him is their ability to get the help they need. To add insult to injury, these same people walk past this crippled man, with no sympathy. They do not offer the assistance he is desperately in need of.

The man and the people I'm talking about are at the pool of Bethesda. I've often wondered what was going through his mind that day. Did he know he was about to have a miraculous encounter that would change his life forever? Did he know he was about to be part of an unforgettable legacy of God's goodness? I assume not but what I am confident about is that everything ordinary about him at that time; every tradition and his acceptance of his condition was completely transformed. Here's the text from the Bible:

"After these things, there was a feast of the Jews; and Jesus went up to Jerusalem. Now there is in Jerusalem by the sheep gate a pool, which is called in Hebrew Bethesda, having five porches. In these lay a multitude of them that were sick, blind, halt, withered. waiting for the moving of the water. (For an angel of the Lord went down at certain seasons into the pool, and troubled the water: whosoever then first after the troubling of

the waters stepped in was made whole, with whatsoever disease he was holden). And a certain man was there, who had been thirty and eight years in his infirmity. When Jesus saw him lying and knew that he had been now a long time in that case, he saith unto him, Wouldst thou be made whole? The sick man answered him, Sir, I have no man, when the water is troubled, to put me into the pool: but while I am coming, another stepped down before me. Jesus saith unto him, Arise, take up thy bed, and walk. And straightway the man was made whole, and took up his bed and walked. Now it was the Sabbath on that day."
(John 5:2-9 ASV)

Have you ever felt crippled by your life? This man's life resembles the lives of many people around the world. They may not all have illnesses, they may not all be poor, but they certainly can relate to this man. People can also identify with the other people who had illnesses and weren't concerned with helping this man to receive his wholeness. There has to be something broken or fractured inside a person who can help but is unwilling to offer help. On one hand, you have a man that can't take the necessary steps toward healing. On the other hand, some people aren't willing to help him take those necessary steps, because they have their own steps to take. These two categories of people are desperately in need of healing. Although this man couldn't walk, he wasn't the only one who needed healing.

"The service you do for others is the rent you pay for your room here on earth."
–Muhammad Ali

I wrote this book because I have felt the burnout. I have seen leaders and peers suffer from the normalcy of tradition where we forget the vision and passion of the purpose that once flamed our hearts. We live in a society where we cover our wounds and mask our scars, yet, we are like that man, desperately in need of a healing touch. You are not alone! There's a desperate need for truth in these times as people pursue society's definition of success. If you could see with spiritual eyes, you would see so many people bent over and crippled by the burdens of life.

The ability to walk upright when you feel as though life is crippling you is a critical step along the journey. As I have mentioned, one of the most misunderstood words in the world is success. Success, alongside money, power, achievements, and just about anything else popular opinion or society wants to throw into the mix have been misunderstood. True success is service to others and this is one of the first things we will discuss in this book.

"In that hour came the disciples unto Jesus, saying, Who then is greatest in the kingdom of heaven? And he called to him a little child, and set him in the midst of them, and said, Verily I say unto you, Except ye turn, and become as little children, ye shall in no wise enter into the kingdom of heaven. Whosoever, therefore, shall humble himself as this little child, the same is the greatest in the kingdom of heaven. And whoso shall receive one such little child in my name receiveth me."
(Matthew 18:1-5 ASV)

Get ready for a supernatural encounter as you read this book. When you walk with God, there is kinetic energy that moves us into the realm of the extraordinary. In Undo Ordinary, I will show you how to live a free, excited and enthusiastic lifestyle. I will show how to be led by God's Spirit and how to take time to parenthetically pause and hear the voice of God. Then, you won't feed the internal compulsions of selfishness. For there is a root of sinful self-interest in all of us that is at odds with being a light in a world filled with darkness. Just as light is incompatible with darkness, the Holy Spirit is incompatible with selfishness. Therefore, we must choose to be led by the Spirit and escape the erratic compulsions of a law-dominated ordinary existence. We must remove the chains of our past.

In life, we often use the past as a source of the pain that we unconsciously try to not deal with. I find it interesting how we construct our thoughts and define ourselves based on the circumstances and situations we've endured. Oftentimes, our past is in a dysfunctional screenplay. We have become actors in a world where dysfunction is the norm, although,

...you have to now use your past as a place of reference and not a place of residence.

we wish we can undo some of the things that we consciously or involuntarily participated in.

We repeat this screenplay over and over again in our minds, making it difficult to move forward. The challenge now becomes: how do we undo the past and more importantly, how do we undo the pain? The answer is, you have to now use your past as a place of reference and not a place of residence. There's an extraordinary life waiting for you on the other side of your pain. Get ready to undo ordinary and step into the fullness of your extraordinary purpose.

Introduction

Every stage of life throws something at you that can be hard to recover from and sometimes, these things may bring you close to death. The Apostle Paul calls these things an adversary to our lives.[1] These adversaries come to hinder us where God has opened a door of opportunity. God is not the only person concerned with our progress in life. Satan is also concerned with our progress and he does everything in his power to stop us from walking in our God-given purpose.

In his writing of the scriptures, Paul noted several encounters with adversity in his walk with God. From people to places to things, there always seemed to be something that tried to keep Paul from achieving what Jesus commissioned him to do.

"And when we were escaped, then we knew that the island was called Melita. And the barbarians showed us no common kindness; for they kindled a fire, and received us all, because of the present rain, and because of the cold. But when Paul had gathered a bundle of sticks and laid them on the fire, a viper came out by reason of the heat, and fastened on his hand. And when the barbarians saw the venomous creature hanging from his hand, they said one to another, No doubt this man is a murderer, whom, though he hath escaped from the sea, yet Justice hath not suffered to live. Howbeit he shook off the creature into the fire, and took no harm. But they expected

---

1 Corinthians 16:9

that he would have swollen, or fallen down dead suddenly: but when they were long in expectation and beheld nothing amiss came to him, they changed their minds, and said that he was a god." (Acts 28: 1-5 ASV)

In this account, Paul writes about his terrible experiences with the shipwreck and the snakebite. These events were back to back and probably, happened all on the same night. During these events, Paul would have lost his life, however, His divine blessing and protection gave him an escape from death. Have you ever felt as though your life was a wreck? We've all had moments in our lives where it seemed as though everything was falling apart all at the same time. Without warning, life happens, leaving you in a place of uncertainty. Have you ever experienced hardships almost simultaneously? Did you survive these events and live to tell it? While you're reading this, you might even still be recovering from a shipwreck and a snakebite, but I have good news for you, you survived it. When a snake bites you, its goal is to put the venom he has inside of you and hurt you. The venom is the poisonous part that immobilizes your body. The poison in the venom from the snake bite damages your central nervous system and paralyzes you completely.

Unfortunately, these events happen to us all in many different ways, oftentimes, they immobilize us. One person's wreck could be divorce and another person could be termination from a job. One person's experience of a bite could come as the result of generational curses brought on by the sins of forefathers or a rough patch in a friendship. It could also be the loss of a dear friend.

On a particular Sunday in January 2017, my best friend for over 30 years, Jason, called me after I preached. He had listened to my sermon online and called to congratulate me on my thorough explanation of the topic. He explained that he didn't feel his best but listened to me preach and felt uplifted. He further explained that as my best friend, one of the most powerful times we shared was when we studied the Bible together in preparation for his deacon ordination.

As we conversed, he continued to encourage me by reaffirming the impact of my preaching and how God was using me in mighty ways. I remember hearing the excitement in his voice and it encouraged me because it was one of those sermons where I wondered if I reached anyone. He went on to state that he wanted me to preach at his funeral because no one knew him like I did. He even told his wife that he wanted me to preach his funeral as well. I expressed to him how much I appreciated his feedback, however, I really didn't want to discuss or even think about preaching his funeral. We had plenty of life left to live before we had to think about that. I quickly changed the subject and asked him for feedback with regards to what should I have done differently. He cut me off mid-sentence and said something so profound. He said: "It doesn't matter what I think, you just keep letting God use you."

I thanked him again and we concluded the conversation and made plans to continue our conversation the following day. The next morning, I woke up to a voice mail from his wife stating that he had been rushed to the hospital at 3:00am. My best friend had a stroke and he was admitted to the hospital. When I went to the hospital and walked into the ICU room, he was heavily sedated and unconscious. He had tubes all over his body and all I could do was fight off my tears. I had to be strong for his family. As I watched him lay there fighting for his life, I felt immense pressure. I watched as his health went up and down like a roller coaster. He was diagnosed with high blood pressure, congestive heart failure, and diabetes.

As if that wasn't bad enough, he was in the hospital for a month, in and out of consciousness. His wife and I switched shifts to be by his side. As I sat by his bedside, I would pray with him, talk to him and squeeze his hand to let him know I was there. Deep down inside, I felt so helpless and broken because my best friend needed me, but I couldn't control the situation. I prayed fervently and I asked God to heal him so we could get back to old times. The doctors told us, as a result of the stroke, over half his brain was damaged and he was going to be in rehab for quite some time.

I remember staring out the window of his room with tears streaming down my face. No one could help ease the horrific pain I was experiencing. I was the minister, the one who people leaned on for answers but here, I was helpless, the one in need for God to perform a miracle.

After a month in the hospital, I received the call from his wife that he had passed away. I was devastated. I thought God went against what I prayed for. I prayed every day for his healing. I never thought the end of his suffering would amount to death.

As I talked to his wife, she reminded me of Jason's desire to have me preach at his funeral. I immediately thought that I was in too much pain to put together a sermon. I needed God's strength more than ever. I felt so alone because I had no one to turn to for help. I tried to write out a sermon but couldn't form complete sentences. There was no clarity in my thoughts because I felt so much pain inside.

As I sat down to find the right words to eulogize my best friend, I had an epiphany. I heard Jason's voice telling me that God was doing some amazing things with me, I just had to keep preaching God's word. It was the last sermon he heard from me, and as his best friend, I felt I had no choice but to carry out his wishes.

Despite the deep loneliness I felt inside, I had to trust God and follow my calling. I preached at his funeral and God moved in a mighty way. On my way home, I cried like never before. I prayed for Jason's healing. At that moment, God reminded me that healing may not always come in how we think it would.

He reminded me that he is the ultimate healer and Jason was in a better place. He was free from pain and in the presence of the one who loved him the most. I was being selfish because I wanted him here. I overlooked the facts that God's ways are not our ways and His thoughts are not our thoughts. Even in the midst of what felt like a personal shipwreck experience, I thanked God for allowing me to encounter one of his angels.

My story may not be the same as yours, and not all of these instances are the same because many different variables can be considered in them all. However, one thing that is the same, across boards; we've all survived! As you read this book, remember that even with everything you've been through, you're still here. And because you're still here, that means there's still an opportunity to have the extraordinary life you were born to live.

Even after a shipwreck, the remains of the ship can be restored and repurposed.

Let's pause for a quick reflection activity.

- What is one shipwreck or snakebite you've experienced in your life?
- How did it impact you?
- Did it create thoughts and perspectives that you didn't have before?
- Would you need to undo them now?

Shipwrecks have purpose wrapped in them. Even after a shipwreck, the remains of the ship can be restored and repurposed.

"Hardship often prepares an ordinary person for an extraordinary destiny."

– Christopher Markus.

"Just because fate doesn't deal you the cards you feel you deserve; it doesn't mean you should give up. It just means you have to play the cards you received to their maximum potential."

– Les Brown

"For God's Word is solid to the core; everything he makes is sound inside and out. He loves it when everything fits when his world is in plumb-line true. Earth is drenched in God's affectionate satisfaction." **(Psalm 33:4-5)**

Trust is not in what you see, but it is having faith in God to show you the possibilities many in life when your eyes are closed.

As we proceed, I'm going to outline and discuss things we can do to survive life's unfortunate events and how you can recover from them by demonstrating and unleashing the power that God has given us as His children. You'll learn a lot about yourself, the people around you, and the people that you will encounter in the future. You weren't born to live an average, ordinary life. God has placed potential, power, and purpose inside of you that the world needs.

"What I know for sure is this: You are built not to shrink down to less but to blossom into more. To be more splendid. To be more extraordinary. To use every moment to fill yourself up."

– Oprah Winfrey

Let's walk together and learn what it means to live beyond where you are right now, move in the power that comes from within and eradicate the process of being ordinary!

Here are a few things that you'll need to know as we walk through this together:

1. You are a Son or Daughter of God. Everything about your life should start from that place and that relational dynamic.
2. You have what it takes! Whether it's already in you or if it's around you and needs to be instilled in you, you certainly have what it takes.

This is a marathon, not a sprint. Enjoy the process of self-discovery and walking in power. As you commit to the process, you will be amazed at how God moves in your life and your relationships. There are eight steps to undoing the ordinary and the number, eight signifies new beginnings.

Welcome to the start of your extraordinary life.

Move Out of Analysis Paralysis

OBJECTIVE:

The objective is to see you develop a forward mentality. It is to see you rise above places and things that do not serve your purpose or future. We start with a biblical example that highlights the traits of stagnation and then I assist you in identifying the power that resides in you.

"Jesus saith unto him, Arise, take up thy bed, and walk. And straightway the man was made whole, and took up his bed and walked." **(John 5:8-9)**

My grandmother was intrigued by the thought of traveling the world. She always wanted to travel but never had the chance to because she had kids at an early age. Each time I traveled with my job, she would ask me about my travel experiences. I would be very descriptive. I was traveling internationally, and I had the opportunity to see the world. I was eager to give her an idea of each place I visited. I told my grandmother once that I had just come from Singapore on a twenty-two-hour flight. She was amazed that I could endure that amount of time on a plane and not go crazy. She told me one of the most profound things I've heard in life. She said, "Son, I see you have traveled a long way. However, the hardest and longest journey you will ever take in life is the one from your head to your heart." Although I was intrigued by the metaphor, I couldn't resist wondering how I could take it and apply it to my life?

During that time, I was struggling with forgiving people who had hurt me. I also had immense anger and indecisiveness with my career. No matter how hard I tried or how willing I was, I could not figure out how to move forward and make some changes in those areas of my life. How do you move forward mentally when you are not sure of what to do to make progress? Could this be the journey my grandmother was talking about? I, soon, realized that she was referring

A man that refuses to change has accepted complicity and is in the cohorts of his own demise.

to the journey of getting outside of your head, believing in your heart that you can let go of the past and running full speed into your future.

God knew I needed His guidance and used my grandmother's counsel to fortify me in a manner that would stay with me for years to come. It was time for me to take up my bed and walk. It was time for me to break away from what had become the norm in my life. I didn't know how I would begin this process, but what I did know was having a mindset for change was the breeding ground for change to manifest. A man that refuses to change has accepted the complicity and is in the cohorts of his own demise.

The phrase, "take up your bed and walk," has echoed for many years. When we hear this statement, it is easy to only consider the man's healing from the condition of lameness. However, his healing was more holistic. Healing infirmity is certainly something that we should attribute to the ministry of Jesus. However, this is not all that Jesus restored within the lame man. Beyond that, faith and right perspective was also given to this man. There weren't just physical limitations that hindered him. His mental capacity was handicapped as well. It required a healing, an undoing.

Jesus didn't address his physical condition directly. Although he was lame, Jesus made no mention of the fact that he couldn't walk. He simply asked him if he would like to be made whole. The response that the man gives lets us know that physical limitations are not all that this man struggled with.[1] He, obviously or maybe not so obviously, had a sense of interdependence and knew that he needed help. But like many people who need help, instead of asking for it, the lame man complained about what he needed.

Let's be very clear about something here. Asking for help and complaining that you have no help are not the same. The former puts you in the position to receive. It opens your heart to the possibility of getting what you need. Complaining leaves you captive to the thing you need. You have been created to have dominion on the earth, that's the kind of power that's at work in you. Anything that has dominion and rule over you, except for God, is out of order and alignment with God's purpose for you. One thing that we, sons and daughters of God, fail to realize is that we are answers and solutions to the challenges people face on earth.[2] With that mindset, a person's complaint ultimately reveals a lack of identity as a son of God. It shows a mindset that requires an upgrade. A child asks for his/her father's help. Don't ever forget who you are. You're a child of God before you are anything else.

When God told the lame man to pick up his bed and walk. He did so with an understanding of who the man was, despite the condition that had become ordinary for him. I believe that this was a divine moment of God to activate

---

1 John 5:7
2 Romans 8:19

the power that was already inside of the man, to get him from where he was to where he could be. The lame man's condition had become the norm; it had become 'the ordinary.' The intervention from Jesus was to assist him in undoing that. Unfortunately, I'm not too sure that the man understood the magnitude of what Jesus instructed him to do. It was time for him to step out of the place of being stuck and he was unsure if he was able to do so. This could have everything to do with the fact that he didn't believe in his heart that he could move forward. He had become so familiar with being lame that he struggled with the ability to believe that things could change. I want to ask you: does this feeling seem familiar to you? Has there ever been a time when the thoughts of your mind have kept you stagnant?

Moving in Greatness

I remember a time when I was going through one of the roughest times of my life. I called my mother and told her that I did not know if I could go on. I remember explaining to her that I was going through a contentious divorce, my business was failing, my kids were hurting because they resented the fact that the family was splitting. To make matters worse, I was asked to take a sabbatical from serving in ministry because my home was out of order. I was having problems medically; I had developed high blood pressure. My doctors couldn't properly diagnose what was going on with my health. They changed my blood pressure medicine over 11 times in the efforts of trying to find the right remedy.

I was having dizzy spells and passed out on a flight while traveling on a business trip. I was overwhelmed by what my life had become.

I went on to tell my mother that I was mentally and spiritually drained. My mother asked me a powerful question. She asked, "What is God telling you during this time and what is he trying to show you?" Unclear as to where she was going with her questions, I simply replied, "I honestly don't know". She began to tell me a story of how God revealed his plans for me before I was born. She shared with me that she was a teen mom who got pregnant at the age of 18 and didn't know how she was going to support a child.

She made up in her mind that she was going to have an abortion because she didn't see a good future as a single mom with no real job or college education. She explained that she had plans to study at Morris Brown and pursue a wonderful career. She went on to tell me that one day, she got on the bus having pre-meditated on an abortion. As she was heading towards the bus, God spoke to her. She stated that God told her that she could not proceed to the doctors because he had so much planned for her baby. God told her that she had to trust him; He would use her baby in a very powerful way.

As I listened to my mother's story, tears began to flow. I began to hear God telling me, in that moment, that I couldn't give up because he had something great in store for me on the other side of my pain. God reminded me that I needed to complete my work in ministry. I was reminded that my failures did not disqualify me from his purpose and plan for my life. I began to weep because I never thought I was worthy to preach or teach God's word. My past mistakes weighed me down, yet, amid my situation, God was still telling me to actively pursue His will for my life. At the time, it felt like I was going crazy, but that day, I committed to God that I would never stop completing the work he called me to do, despite all odds. I dried my tears and asked Him to renew my strength. I renewed my commitment to Him and asked Him to never stop speaking to me. I thanked God for trusting me and using me in spite of everything I had been through.

You can think yourself into something or out of it.

I also thanked him for a praying mother who was obedient to His voice. Without her obedience, I wouldn't be here today. I am eternally grateful to God for a mother who has exemplified relentless faith. After speaking with my mother, I soon began to realize that the biggest enemy in my life was me. I was failing at life because I failed to value what God placed inside of me.

Although the enemy told me that I was a mistake, God reminded me that I was a conqueror. I discovered that my thoughts were holding me back from walking in victory.

31

My mother's story inspired me during one of the most difficult moments of my life because she didn't allow what seemed to be a hopeless situation to stop her from birthing greatness.

God does not want our thoughts to hinder our progress. He also lets us know that the capacity to move forward starts with your heart and mind. The Bible says in Proverbs 23:7, "For as he thinketh in his heart, so is he: Eat and drink, saith he to thee; but his heart is not with thee." In other words, the thoughts that you think within your heart and rehearse in your mind, have the power to manifest as your reality. You can think yourself into something or out of it. For this reason alone, we need to guard our hearts and screen our thoughts.

There is no way to achieve the extraordinary if you don't think and believe that you can. It must start with the thoughts in your mind before it physically manifests in your life.

Do you believe that things can change in your life?

The process of moving forward starts with a change in thoughts. Don't dwell on what went wrong. Undo the ordinary by focusing on the next steps. It is perfectly fine to assess the situation to understand what created the mistake; however, it is much more productive, rewarding and gratifying to have a plan in place to prevent the mistake from reoccurring in the future. Developing a plan to learn and grow is what God wants for us. The steps to finding the answers are within you and waiting to be unleashed.

"The greatest thing in this world is not so much where we stand, but the direction we are moving in."
        –Johann Wolfgang von Goethe

Here is a challenge for you. Do as God instructed in Habakkuk 2:2: Write the vision and make it plain. You can do this by taking these steps:

1. Develop a purpose and a vision statement for your life.
2. Write down what you want your life to look like.
3. Put a plan in motion to make your goals achievable.

My Purpose Statement

_____

_____

_____

_____

_____

My Vision Statement

_____

_____

_____

_____

_____

Developing S.M.A.R.T goals

Write the vision, make it plain on the table that he may run who reads it.

(Habakkuk 2:2)

Goal setting is a critical part of actionable change. Nothing great, that was ever created, was achieved without a carefully thought out plan. Goals are a means to an end. I put in X amount of work because I want to see Y in the future. It is what gets you up early in the morning. It is that which gives you the drive to fulfill your purpose. Goals shape our lives, they create our destiny. If there were no goals, our world would be so chaotic but even more so, we would never fully know the potential.

> Nothing great, that was ever created, was achieved without a carefully thought out plan.

Most people feel a certain kind of pressure or tension on New Year's Day. They write down their goals for the year but after a few months, they neglect them. This is because there is a common misconception of goal setting. It is not enough to write down the goals. What are the daily, precise, fundamental decisions you are making to reach that goal? Most people aren't consistent because they are not sure of the 'why.' Purpose is better than outcome. Why are you setting these goals?

There is a pressure and a tension that comes with goal setting. It stems from a dissatisfaction with where you are versus where you want to be. These are primary drivers of human action. Take advantage of it. Make it real and imagine you already got it.

What is S.M.A.R.T goal setting?

S.M.A.R.T goal setting is simply giving your goals a precise structure and an estimable attainability. Now, what do I mean by this? Ever had a situation where you say to yourself, "I want to own my car at the end of the year," and when the end of the year rolls out, you realize you haven't met that goal? Well, that's probably because it was not a S.M.A.R.T goal.

When setting goals, you need to devise an outline of how you hope to reach that goal. There are decisions you have to make every day to get to that point. S.M.A.R.T goals help you set up realistic goals because you get the opportunity to analyze and evaluate the reasons behind those goals and how they can be achieved.

This framework works in both the corporate and personal settings. You can use S.M.A.R.T goals to become a better mother or father. You can also use S.M.A.R.T to get that promotion at work. It's all up to you.

What does the S.M.A.R.T goal stand for?

Simply put, the S.M.A.R.T goal stands for Specific,

Measurable, Attainable, Relevant and Time- Specific goals. These are important to reach certain milestones in your personal and corporate lives.

SPECIFIC

Time to get down to the specifics. It is what sets you apart from the person who says "I want to be a billionaire but doesn't put into writing how they're going to get there. Get down to the nitty-gritty descriptions of how you want to attain your goals.

Ask yourself questions like What? Why? When? How? Where? Who? What are the reasons, resources, conditions, limitations or the options you have to achieve that goal? Is this goal feasible?

MEASURABLE

You may be wondering, how do I measure my goals? Well, this is pretty simple. Divide your large goal into sub-set goals. For instance, I want to become a fashion designer. I would need to create sub-goals to attain this. What are people doing to achieve this? I have to launch my website, define my brand, layout a few articles up on my website, gather client testimonials and get leads in my pipeline via email. By doing this, I have made this goal measurable. I can go back to my list and tick off the sub-goals I have attained. These sub-goals serve as milestones. The amount of satisfaction and dopamine that comes from ticking things off your list is immeasurable.

ATTAINABLE

A goal is attainable when it is realistic. A realistic goal would be measured using the available resources (time, cost, materials, efforts). For instance, I want to lose 15 pounds in 20 weeks. This is an attainable goal. I can achieve it by changing my diet and taking a walk for an hour every day. If I keep at it, I may just lose 15 pounds in 18 weeks.

You can also use the effort and value matrix to measure an attainable goal. Usually, the goals with the least effort and the most value are easy to attain. They are, therefore, the most realistic. If I want to write a blog post every day, I just need to set aside 2-3 hours of my day. What are the realistic goals you've set in the past?

RELEVANT

This is the part where I ask you what your idea of success is. Do you want to be an insta blogger? Do you want to be a famous YouTube vlogger? Do you want to be a responsible parent? Or perhaps, you want to own the world's largest oil mill. Your idea of success will determine the significance of your goal.

What are your reasons behind the goals you are setting for yourself? An example would be, "I want to be a famous YouTube vlogger so that way I can quit my regular day job, develop financial freedom, have fun and spend time with my loved ones. Understanding the relevance of your goal would motivate you to keep working until you attain a height you are satisfied with. The desire for financial freedom can keep you focused. It can prompt you to wake up early in the morning or keep you late at night. If you can see it, then, you can reach it. Dream big and aim high.

TIME BOUND

You know what they say, "Time is money." You have to know the value of your time. Once you know the value of your time, you will be more careful about where, how and with whom you spend your time.

Time can be an effective tool in setting personal/corporate goals. I can say, "I want to earn a million dollars in a year," but if there's no time or accountability partner attached to it, I may never reach this goal. It would be better to say, "I want to earn $600,000 in revenue by next year, December 2020." To get $600, 000 in a year in revenue, I need to earn $50,000 a month. I need to make a

Awareness of who you are and where you are is critical to achieving your goals.

detailed plan on earning $12,500 every week in revenue till December 2020. I can even get a partner to keep me accountable so by December 2020, I attain that goal.

Time is a great resource. If it is used wisely, it can bring enormous dividends.

EXERCISE:

Now that you know about S.M.A.R.T goals, what plans do you have that you can apply S.M.A.R.T goals to? List them below:

_____

_____

_____

_____

_____

_____

The Power of Awareness

Now that your S.M.A.R.T goals are written down, let's shift to the topic of awareness. These are probably rhetorical questions I'm about to ask, but reflect on them anyway. Have you ever been completely oblivious to something about yourself that others could see? Or have others been oblivious to things that you see in yourself? I don't think the first question applies to the lame man in John chapter 5, but I do think the second question applies to him. As I mentioned earlier, this man was very aware of the fact that he needed assistance. Even if his way of conveying that was skewed, he was still aware. Awareness of who you are and where you are is critical to achieving your goals. A person's awareness of where they are in life is the first step toward preparation for the progress they want to make. I say preparation is because simply being aware of something doesn't mean that you have movement or momentum.

Awareness of location or condition is one thing, moving and making the necessary adjustments in your daily life is another. Let's explore the power of awareness.

The CAMEL Power

There is one powerful animal in the Bible that teaches us about awareness. The camel is an animal that was used frequently in biblical days as a means of transportation. The camel has several characteristics that will help us in understanding the concept of awareness.

1. **The ability to have vision:** The camel is usually in the desert for an extensive amount of time and goes on long trips. It has to deal with the elements of dust and dirt and is challenged by a vision-impairing environment. With all of these obstacles, what is protecting the camel? Remarkably, camels have 3 eyelids that protect the cornea and eyes as a whole. The camel can also see predators from long distances which is

   He has shown me that a diet will change how you look, but a fast will change how you see.

   important for their protection. Figuratively speaking, the eyelids signify the vision God has given us in life. The number 3 represents the trinity biblically, so we can say the 3 eyelids signify the Father, Son, and the Holy Spirit. When we move in power, we operate in a capacity of clear vision. We may lose our patience, but we must never lose our hope. We sometimes lose our sight, but we must never lose our vision. We sometimes lose our way, but we must never lose our purpose. We sometimes lose our temper, but we must never lose our temperance. We sometimes lose people we thought we needed, but we must never lose our faith in God. With all the things we can lose in life, we must never lose our ability to see God in every situation.

2. **The ability to fast:** There are two different types of camels: the Dromedary camel (the kind that has only one hump) and the Bactrian camel (the kind that has two humps). The camel stores food and water in the humps. Their humps allow them to store up to 80 pounds of fat which they can live off for weeks and even months! They can fast during their journey. We must fast to take the time to strengthen our relationship with God. In my time of speaking with God, He has shown me that a diet will change how you look, but a fast will change how you see.

3. **The ability to pray:** Camels can comfortably sit in very hot sand, thanks to the thick pads of skin on their chest and knees. Their kneeling can be synonymous with praying. As believers, we must be able to get on our knees and pray in the hottest situations.

"And pray in the Spirit on all occasions with all kinds of prayers and requests. With this in mind, be alert and always keep on praying for all the Lord's people." **(Ephesians 6:18)**

The camel helps us facilitate our awareness of our surroundings and our ability to spend time with God. We must be deliberate and intentional in spending time with God and hearing from Him. Have you ever tried to pray and your prayers get distracted by other thoughts and your mind wanders off? Have you ever tried to pray and instantly fall asleep? Distractions can be very dangerous. It is like texting and driving. It is like going to church and talking during the sermon. Driving and texting can kill you and others. Likewise, talking during church can cause you to miss God's word. The distractions during your prayers are the very things in your life that impede your direct contact with God. There are times where you must isolate yourself with God and remove all distractions.

The awareness of help is what I think Jesus recognized in this man in the scripture. A man who lacked faith, hope, and courage, yet, still had awareness in his heart. You see, even in despair, we still have something in us that God can pull from and use for our restoration. When Jesus asked this man if he would be made whole, He was letting us know that he knew this man was aware. One of the things you'll continue to find out as you walk with God is that you're not always aware of what you need based on your condition, but the moment you become self-aware, God can begin to alter your perspective and bring what you know into proper alignment with His word and His will for your life.

In this story, I find the indifference of the people around him very interesting. Although the people knew something was wrong with him (probably because the place was known for people will illnesses of all kinds), they never helped him get in the pool, like the rest of the people receiving healing. As a result, they walked right by him. They weren't concerned with helping, they were more concerned about their ailments. They had their own needs that needed to be met. In a lot of ways we could call this selfishness, however, we have to consider the traits of everyone in this environment. They were in survival mode and people in this state of mind aren't interested in what others have going on.

The Power of Agreement

There are two types of agreement that I want to focus on. I chose to highlight these two agreements because you can't have one without having the other. They work in tandem to create the balance a person needs when, just like Paul, they have been shipwrecked or snake-bitten and need to recover. These agreements serve as a first aid kit and CPR when life seems to get the best of us. You can count on these two agreements to breathe life into the dream and the dreamer when dead dreams need to be revived. When a person has stagnated in their pursuit of achieving the goals they have set, you can count on these agreements to push a person past the place that they have plateaued.

I'm sure there are other ways to recover from bad experiences because there's more than one way to do something right.

For the sake of this discussion, these two are the most relevant, I hope you see why.

Relational Agreement

"The sick man answered him, Sir, I have no man, when the water is troubled, to put me into the pool: but while I am coming, another steps down before me." **(John 5:7 ASV)**

When people are wounded or hurting, they often feel alone. This can immediately thrust a person into survival mode. At that moment, everything is about self and rightfully so. If there is a wounded person who is not concerned about tending to his/her wound, you might want to check their pulse or check to see if they're in shock. "I have no man" is probably one of the most repeated and echoed sentiments in human history. We were created to desire companionship and partnership. We were not designed to do life alone. It was certainly never meant for us to heal in isolation or deal with hardships without the help and care of our neighbors.

From the moment we are conceived in our mother's womb, we have someone at our side, walking with us through life. And God would have it that way because He said, "it is not good for man to be alone." In the lame man's complaint and response to Jesus, he knew he needed some type of relationship to get him to the pool. I have highlighted the importance of developing relationships with people that can help you get to your destination. According to God's word, you are supposed to be healed and others around you are supposed to help you receive your healing.

I want to point out that though the man in our text initially had no one to help him get into the pool to be healed, God will always send someone to assist you. Not only will they come to assist you, but they will ask the right questions and say the things you need to hear even if they are different from what you want to hear. These same people will challenge how you see yourself and how you see the world around you. Often times, a flawed perspective of self and a limited worldview can cause a person to spend many years in the same place without ever progressing toward the future God has for them.

Theological Agreement

I woke up one morning and realized the middle toe on my right foot was hurting. I could not remember how it happened, but it appeared to be broken. I went to the emergency room for x-rays to see the extent of my injuries. I saw the doctor; he said that it was not broken, but I needed buddy tape. He said he would tape the bad toe to the good toe. By taping both toes, the bad toe would adopt the characteristics of the good toe. It was later explained that by taping those toes together, it would help in the movement, flexibility, and development of the bad toe. That day, I learned a powerful life lesson. The things we are attached to determine or help facilitate our level of healing and development.

When conjoined twins are born, in most instances, they are unable to survive or function without each other, but because they're attached and share the same heart, they're able to survive. We as believers in Christ must attach ourselves to God's word. The word of God will facilitate our healing process and serve as our survival guide for life.

I mentioned theological agreement earlier. I am willing to bet that you thought I meant you had to sit and debate scripture with someone until you both came to an agreement, but that's far from my intention. Having knowledge and becoming acquainted with God's word concerning your life are necessities for every aspect of your life. God's word is eternal and has been in existence before our lives were formed and will remain after our lives cease to exist. The Word of God is what brings us into alignment with His will and purpose for us. His word is what He used to create the earth. He even went as far as making His word form into flesh, becoming who we know as our Lord and Savior Jesus Christ. That's how important God's Word is. That's how much regard and reverence He wants us to give to His Word. Whether it be His written word, spoken or revealed word (prophecy), agreement with God's word should be a top priority.

Before we discussed relational agreement, we talked about how the two types of agreements that work in tandem with each other. In our discussion of the relational agreement, we learned that God doesn't desire for us to be alone or do life separate from Him or other people. We know that because He said it multiple times. I'll like to end this chapter with all that God says about relational agreement. I believe if we do this, your heart will begin to line up with God's word and intent for you to live by the power of His word, which is a step you should always be willing to take toward your future.

The Word of God is what brings us into alignment with His will and purpose for us.

ROMANS 8:19 - "For the earnest expectation of the creation waiteth for the revealing of the sons of God."

You are a son or daughter of God which means that you have others that are a part of your kingdom family. These are people that you should be developing relationships with.

EPHESIANS 4:29 - Let no corrupt speech proceed out of your mouth, but such as is good for edifying as the need may be, that it may give grace to them that hear.

What you say and what is said to you makes a difference in the quality of your life.

Galatians 6:1 - Brethren, even if a man be overtaken in any trespass, ye who are spiritual, restore such a one in a spirit of gentleness; looking to thyself, lest thou also be tempted.

When you are feeling down, your recovery is heavily

dependent on who lifts you from that low place. This means not everyone around you has the Holy Spirit or the ability to restore you.

Proverbs 11:14 - Where no wise guidance is, the people falleth; But in the multitude of counselors there is safety.

In your hurt, guidance from those around you is vital to your healing.

Genesis 2:18 - And Jehovah God said, It is not good that the man should be alone; I will make him a help meet for him.

God never intended for us to do life without Him and other people. If you are isolated or tend to isolate yourself from others, you put yourself at risk of staying in a place of hurt or even stagnation. You don't do life alone! You're not built for it!

Your inability to analyze, determine, decide, and move forward are all wrapped up in a neglect of the right relationships with people and the Word of God. These are two powers that you can move in that will help you stay fit in the mold and shape of God's purpose for you.

When I was growing up, I would work in the yard with my dad, although I was not really excited about working in the yard with him. I enjoyed having the time for us to talk and just kind of have our man talks. I would share my thoughts and dreams with him, and I would always conclude by asking him what he thought. He would always keep working and seemingly not pay attention to me. One day, I asked him about his thoughts on my dreams of driving a truck, owning a trucking company, and playing professional basketball. He told me if I became a truck driver or a basketball player, I would not eat either of my grandmother's cooking during the holidays. I was immediately discouraged and stated that I would not do the truck driving because I thought that was not worth missing either of my grandmothers' cooking. He looked me in the eyes and said, "Don't you ever let anyone talk you out of your dreams." He explained that I don't need anyone to validate my dreams. He said, "Don't give blind people permission to proofread your vision." The most compelling words he said were, "God gives you visions and dreams, and they are not for everyone to see." I realized that we often don't move because either we talk ourselves out of our dreams or we let others do it. Follow your dreams and visions, regardless of what they are. Don't be moved by what others think or say. Some people live for the validation of others while others live in condemnation. When you stop living in the guilt of your past, you free yourself from the prison of shame. You finally realize that you have been pardoned by the one who matters the most, your Heavenly father. Your current situation is not your final destination.

KEY TWO

Move on the Soul Train

OBJECTIVE:

To facilitate growth and help you understand what is required to move into a new realm.

"What is a soul? It's like electricity- we don't really know what it is, but it's a force that can light a room."

— Ray Charles

[1] THE LORD is my Shepherd to feed, guide, and shield me, I shall not lack. [2] He makes me lie down in fresh, tender green pastures;

He leads me beside the still and restful waters. [3] He refreshes and restores my life (myself); He leads me in the paths of righteousness uprightness and right standing with Him--not for my earning it, but for His name's sake. [4] Yes, though I walk through the deep, sunless valley of the shadow of death, I will fear or dread no evil, for You are with me; Your rod to protect and Your staff to guide, they comfort me. [5] You prepare a table before me in the presence of my enemies. You anoint my head with oil; my brimming cup runs over. [6] Surely or only goodness, mercy, and unfailing love shall follow me all the days of my life, and through the length of my days the house of the Lord and His presence shall be my dwelling place. **(Psalm 23:1-6 AMPC)**

Emotional Movement

Narayana Murthy says, "Growth is painful, change is painful, but nothing is more painful than being stuck where you don't belong." When a person is emotionally retarded, we offer therapy. When a person experiences physical retardation, we offer physical therapy. However, when we are spiritually retarded, we neglect it and act like we have no problem and make no

An extraordinary life is a life that is sold out for God.

investment in trying to receive healing from our spiritual depletion. Retardation, in this context, means a state of being stagnant or stuck. Matthew verse 16:25-25 says,

"Whosoever desires to save his life must lose it. Whoever loses his life for my sake will find it." When we selfishly love our own life more than we love God, who gave us life, we leave ourselves open to the attacks of the enemy.

In Revelation 12:11, it says that they overcame Satan by 2 things:
   1. By the words of their testimony, and
   2. They love not their lives even until death.

Through this scripture, we see that loving your life leaves space for the devil to infiltrate. Sometimes we can love people, material things, and our success more than we love God. You have to get the point where the devil tries to devour you but has nothing to hold onto. Why, because your life in so hidden in Christ that he can't even get to you. An extraordinary life is a life that is sold out for God.

In Genesis, the Bible says God made the serpent wiser than any animal in the garden. When the serpent tricked Eve, God caused it to eat the dust of the earth forever. God told the serpent that as long as it lived, it would crawl on its belly and eat the dust of the earth. However, God made man out of the dust of the earth. As long as you are operating in the flesh, the devil has a legal right to devour you. Therefore, when we stop emotionally and spiritually moving in the direction God planned for our lives, it is at that very moment we succumb to Satan's plan by actively stunting our emotional and spiritual growth.

For many people, there seems to be something they struggle with through a life-time that constantly nags them. For some people, it's a curse of debt and poverty. For some, it's a wayward child. For others, it's a struggle with favorable and unfavorable circumstances that affects them mentally, physically, and emotionally. Unfavorable events usually accompany trauma and woundedness. Trauma doesn't necessarily mean that something traumatic like death or a near-death injury or sickness experience has taken place. Depending on how a person's mind calculates and processes life events, something such as a bad breakup could be considered traumatic for someone. Anything that negatively affects and damages the psychological, emotional, or physical makeup of a person can be considered as an agent of trauma. One could even argue that trauma is relative to the experience of an individual. This means that what is traumatic to one person may not be traumatic to another. Again, it mostly depends on how a person's mind processes things.

David was a person who experienced rejection from his father, was mocked and jeered at by his older brothers, had fights with a bear, a lion, and an actual giant. He probably had quite a bit of trauma. I'm almost sure of it, actually. As a person who consistently had people trying to kill him, experienced the death of his newborn child and had his son rape his daughter, David experienced more trauma than many of us would ever imagine. I would dare to say that David probably got to a point where he expected trauma.

In addition to external trauma, David had to deal with his own internal struggles. Throughout his life, David made bad choices, including giving in to lust by sleeping with Bathsheba. He had to face external consequences for his actions because of an internal struggle. David had to live with the consequences of a bad decision.

Have you ever dealt with the aftermath of a bad decision? Perhaps, you feel your life would be a lot better if you made the right choices. Perhaps, you wake up wondering if you chose the right career, partner, or business deal. Or perhaps, you live with the pain of regret from bad decisions that have left an indelible mark on your life. You feel stuck, as though you can't move past the internal trauma it has caused.

When you've endured numerous traumatic experiences, it trains you. In other words, cycles of trauma can shape everything concerning you: how you see yourself, how you see others, what you expect from life and situations, and so on. Much like David, many of us have been through a lot. In more ways than one, our unfortunate experiences have done some damages to us. But guess what? It's repairable. The damage can be reversed. David had trauma, yet he was still a king. David made bad decisions, yet he was still a king. And just like David had a God-ordained purpose despite his flaws, so do you.

The King was a damaged person with an extensive history of bad experiences. However, this didn't stop him from acknowledging that he possessed something that helped him deal with the trauma. He realized that he had much more around him and in him to look forward than what life and bad choices had brought him. He had the help of his Lord, the one he worshiped, the one who the Bible says had his heart. He had a deep and intimate relationship with God. Although his emotional, mental, and physical health were most times at risk, he had a connection with someone who made things stable and gave him focus. When David was with God, he was at his best. Time in God's presence was the best part of David's narrative consistently. He was the best version of himself that he could be whenever He encountered God. He was the son, father, king, warrior, prophet, and psalmist that God created him to be.

I believe that the one thing that benefited David the most was his understanding of his soul, his mind, his will, and his emotions. We must be like David in this regard as it pertains to our own lives. Without complete dependence on God, David's soul would have remained in a state of ruin. This had already become ordinary (normal) for him.

When David felt depleted, his first response was to go to God and allow himself to go on a journey with Him. This journey was comprised of David's acknowledgment that he needed a helper. He would then transition to what his helper prompted him to do. The thing that David would not do himself, he surrendered them to the wisdom and protection of God. The next part of his journey would consist of David explaining how God would restore him in ways that no one else could. David recognized he needed God to chart his path. We must recognize that we are not in control. We must learn to relinquish our desire to be in control. For some of us, this is a huge feat. To undo our past patterns of behavior, we have to follow David's example.

Before you continue reading, I want to offer you a huge tip that I believe will not only aid in undoing the ordinary but also help to facilitate a healthy new normal:

PURSUE THE PRESENCE OF GOD INTENTIONALLY, AND REGULARLY.

This was one of David's tools in life. He understood that everything—especially the healing and newness he desperately needed—for his life could be found in the presence of God. Now, it is absolutely okay to have some practical means by which you cope and deal with life, such as counseling, venting to trusted friends, activities that are therapeutic, and so on. However, we cannot forsake and forget about spiritual things. **Spiritual + practical = the best approach.** Always bear this in mind. It will certainly carry you throughout life.

Get On Board

The problem a lot of people struggle with is getting into the Rocking Chair Syndrome. The thing about a rocking chair is that it goes back and forth but never goes anywhere.

We find ourselves doing a lot of movement in life but never really going anywhere, or remaining stagnant. We feel that there has to be more to life than the routine: working, taking care of the kids, paying bills, and ultimately feeling under accomplished. Therefore, you have to take control of your

It doesn't make us perfect, yet, it perfects us daily.

life and make sure that you do things that help execute movement.

David expressed how God led him and how God had control of his life. Much like a conductor of a moving train, God ordered David's starts and stops – his times of aggressive movement and his much-needed rest. This brings us to the title of this chapter, "Move on the Soul Train."

The Right Track

"He makes me lie down in fresh, tender green pastures; He leads me beside the still and restful waters." **(Psalm 23:2)**

Because we don't always make the best decisions, God makes sure that we get what we need and also get where we need to be, when we live a life submitted to Him. This is why total submission to God is so important. In His loving-kindness and grace, He hides our mistakes and grants us righteousness. The grace of God keeps us in good standing. It doesn't make us perfect, yet, it perfects us daily. He even puts us in the position to prosper, sometimes, in ways that we would have never thought of.

Without God, there's a path that we would choose that has little or limited success waiting for us. Without God, we sometimes choose the track that offers us the least amount of progress and traction– a track that is not in alignment with God's will concerning us. There are destinations that we would never reach or arrive at too late.

Have you ever considered how much people rely and depend on others to make sure they are successful? On this journey, who will hold you accountable for moving into a new realm of thinking and doing?

Let's go back to the idea of God being a train conductor. If you've ever been on a train or watched a movie depicting a collection of travelers on a train, you would know that everyone on the train depends on the operator to get them to their destination safely. They pay admission only for them to submit to the personality, training, and will of the train conductor, and more often than not, they reach their destination safely and on time. This is how we should live our lives with God. It's exactly how David lived his life. He paid his admission fee by surrendering his life to the will of God. In doing this, he was led to green pastures where he could get the nourishment he needed and led to still waters where he could receive peace and refreshment.

The Moving Track

I want you to take a spiritual train ride with me for a moment. I think God takes us on the Soul train in the midst of him restoring our soul. This simply implies that one could lose or deplete his or her soul. Sometimes, in our lives, we create a false sense of strength that imprisons us. As a result, many people tend to judge others and most times do so unrighteously. There are a few thoughts on why this is the case. While those that are the recipients of grace should extend grace to others, this is not always the case. Some people choose not to extend grace because they forget the grace and mercy that God has given them. Others are judgmental because they come face-to-face with their past, and it makes looking in the mirror uncomfortable. Hiding our flaws from others with newfound holiness is more comfortable than showing transparency, owning the past, and rejoicing in the testimony of God's grace and mercy. This is what God intended and reiterated in the message in James 5:16. Simply stated, we are to confess our sins to each other so that we may be healed. Those that receive of the Lord should give to the Lord and His people. This is what pleases the heart of God.

Sometimes we judge others and don't give grace, simply because we have forgotten what God is delivering us from. When you remember, you release grace. Notice, I didn't say delivered because we are all in the process of being delivered from something.

Although we would like to believe that we are flawless, we all have an area of our lives that is currently under construction by God. Some of us are not fully delivered from past hurts, situations, and traumas. As a defense mechanism, we prefer to act as though we have it all together as if we have no problems, bills, or hang-ups or insecurities; but all of us struggle with something. Some of us are working out our salvation daily. The truth is, we all should be. We may put on a good show, but we are not there yet. There is no such thing as arrived. It's a consistent journey for us all. This does not mean we are purposely not where we should be, but some of us are struggling, and that's perfectly okay.

If you don't have to work at it or do anything to get it, you won't appreciate it.

"You are allowed to be both a masterpiece and a work in progress, simultaneously."

– Sophia Bush

Struggle teaches appreciation. What you struggle for you also value. If you don't have to work at it or do anything to get it, you won't appreciate it. This also applies to the work of restoration. If you don't have to toil for it, there's no pressure to value it. If there is little to no investment, we can't see the full benefit of it. So, God, sometimes, lets us spend a lifetime struggling with some things to remind us that we always need restoration of our soul.

We, most times, find ourselves dealing with past hurts and the pains of life that have damaged our soul. David was clearly was not a stranger to a damaged soul. The book of Psalms gives us a front-row seat to David's emotional state throughout various stages of his life. This was the same man who had been stuck in a cave for 7 years in Psalms 142 and cried out to the Lord. In the book of Samuel, this was the man whose daughter, Tamar, was raped by her brother, and he dealt with the anger of his child being violated. This was the man who was a peeping Tom and watched Bathsheba, another man's wife, bathe and slept with her. This is a man that had experienced so much guilt that he tried to cover up his actions. This guy, David, clearly had been dealing with a damaged soul at various times in his life. He has gone through periods of his life where he needed God to restore his soul.

What exactly is soul restoration?

To understand soul restoration, we must understand what the soul actually is. Further, we must note the difference between the soul and the spirit. Let's go ahead and define what a soul is. We must not get the soul and spirit confused, although, in the Bible, they are used interchangeably.

Hebrews 4:12 says, "... for the word of God is quick, and powerful, and sharper than any two-edged sword, piercing even to THE DIVIDING ASUNDER OF SOUL AND

SPIRIT, and of the joints and marrow, and is a discerner of the thoughts and intents of the heart".

The Bible clearly makes a distinction between the soul and the spirit. The soul can come in several forms. There are even different uses of the word, 'soul.' The Thomistic/Aristotelian Philosophical usage of it applies to anything which is alive. However, there are three main types of souls: vegetative (mainly in plants), sensitive (mainly in animals), and rational (mainly in humans). Colloquially, "soul" is often used as referring to rational souls. The soul is really anything that is alive and has emotions or feelings.[1]

The spirit is synonymous with the psyche. Most times, when we hear psyche, we think of the human mind. Psyche in Greek means 'breath' or 'breath of life.' The word, 'spirit,' also stems from the Hebrew word for soul, '*chay*' which means 'living or alive.' If you merge the two definitions, it means the soul is living, breathing and alive. In the book of Genesis, man became a living being.

In Romans 8:16, Paul talks of the spirit of man and the Holy Spirit - "*the Spirit himself bears witness with our spirit that we are children of God.*" This is similar to what may happen in the court of law. The Holy Spirit serves as a witness. He provides concrete evidence to our spirit that we are children of the Most High.

---

1 Do animals have souls of some sort?

After the resurrection, Jesus became both spirit and flesh. He could go anywhere at any time because *the spirit is like the wind and goes wherever it pleases* (John 3:8). You may not see the spirit but He is constantly moving.

In Luke 24:39, Jesus tells Philip, *"See my hands and my feet, that it is I myself. Touch me and see. For a spirit does not have flesh and bones as you see that I have."* Even at the well, Jesus tells the Samaritan woman that He was seeking true worshipers who would worship God in spirit and in truth (John 4:24). The human spirit can understand spiritual truths through the Holy Spirit. For we know, we need a Savior who would save us from our sinful and broken nature. It is the Spirit of God that reveals this to us. For no one can come to the Father unless He who sent me draws him.[2]

There is a clear distinction between the soul and the spirit. The spirit is our inner being that connects with God, and the soul is more of the emotional part of who we are; our mind is the state of who we are. The body is the fleshy part of us that makes up our physical being. In this text, we want to focus on the soul. David says that God restores his soul because he is hurting at times and needs for God to restore his emotions and his mind.

Now that we've defined what a soul is and have made a distinction between the spirit and the soul, I want to answer

---

2 John 6:44

the question posed earlier: ***what exactly is soul restoration?***

"The Lord is my shepherd, there is nothing I lack. In green pastures, he makes me lie down; to still waters he leads me; he restores my soul. He guides me along the right paths for the sake of his name." **(Psalm 23:1-3)**

'He restores my soul' means He repairs, renovates our innermost being. He created us so He can fix us no matter how damaged our soul may seem. In the Word of God, we see times when He has given us the wisdom to maneuver through life's challenges. In Timothy 3;16-17, the scripture is God's breath. It is used for teaching, rebuking, and training so that His people may be equipped for what He has called them to do. It can even encourage the faint-hearted and serves as a guide to whoever seeks a life of peace and satisfaction.[3]

Many books say, "Soup for the Soul," or "How to maintain happiness in your home," however, it is only the Word of God that brings total restoration to the soul. Those who are born again experience the peace and joy that comes from the scriptures. This is further attained through salvation and the relationship with God.

Faith is developed by hearing. The Lord has given us His Word to seek strength and encouragement in times of trouble. We

---

3 Psalm 119:97 - 105

can spend time reading His Word[4], praying, and offering our supplications and receiving support from other Christians.[5]

There is a common misconception that believers do not get discouraged. There were many instances when men and women of God faced challenging situations that left them discouraged. The prophet, Elijah, experienced depression after he had heard Jezebel would take his life, and this was after he had called on God to bring down fire on the altar to make a clear statement to the prophets of Baal. There are many remedies in the scriptures. We can take a look at the book of Psalms. King David wrote psalms during trying times in his life. That is why David can say the Lord restores my soul.[6]

Give God room to bring restoration in your life. Let him show you the solution to your problem and let the Holy Spirit minister spiritual truths through His Word. Do you need God to restore some things in your life? Ask yourself these questions:

- Am I in need of restoration?
- How can I create a space of healing that allows me to start afresh?

To receive restoration, you need to accept that God is willing

---

4 Romans 10:17
5 2 Corinthians 1:3-4
6 Psalm 23:3

to restore your soul. You need to take all our heavy burdens to the altar. A lot of believers struggle with certain sins and temptations, but they are not willing to present it to God because they think He cannot be bothered with such trivial issues. Take all your worries and cares to God, and He will answer you. Recognize the value and the worth of being a child of God, unbelievers don't get this privilege.

One of the eye awakening situations of realizing the value of something was dealing with my hobby car. I have a 1968 Oldsmobile Convertible Cutlass that costs $3,200 in 1968. Throughout the years, the vehicle had over 30 years of wear and tear. In 2006, I restored the car with new paint, tires, engine, and electrical wires, etc. Upon having it repaired, I went to have the vehicle appraised for an estimate of its value for insurance purposes. The appraiser explained to me that since I had restored the car back to the original condition, the car was more valuable than it was at the time of the original purchase. He further explained that the car was worth more than $20,000. I will relate this to humanity. Once we realize that God has restored our soul and made us new, we begin to appreciate in value, and we stop giving people discounts of ourselves. We no longer accept anything less than what we feel we deserve. We no longer go places or engage with people that devalue our worth. What was at one point, ordinary and acceptable in my life,

We no longer go places or engage with people that devalue our worth.

now becomes distasteful because I now realize my worth. Do you know your worth? Are you remaining in the mundane when God is ready to take you to extraordinary places?

The Wrong Track

"Yes, though I walk through the deep, sunless valley of the shadow of death, I will fear or dread no evil, for You are with me; Your rod to protect and Your staff to guide, they comfort me." **(Psalm 23:4)**

Remember those bad decisions we discussed earlier? Those made by David? Well, the majority of those were intentional. Although he was in a place he probably shouldn't have been, God was still there with him. Although he chose not to allow God to be his train operator and lead him to this place, God didn't abandon him. That is the most excellent benefit of having a relationship with God. He's always there, always present, and ready to meet you wherever you are and fulfill your needs.

God isn't just present in our times of distress, He's there to bring correction and comfort to us. However, that comfort is contingent upon our perspective concerning corrections. Most people don't like being corrected, and that is essentially a pride issue. If something is out of alignment, then it should be realigned by correction. That is certainly not a bad thing, but what happens in the soul of a prideful person is that their thoughts, will, and emotions are offended and challenged.

Simply put, correction is not comfortable to the prideful. The humility necessary to know that you need correction is what brings comfort to the thoughts, will, and emotions of a person that wants to be positioned, postured, and placed correctly. Otherwise, going down the wrong track, and becoming your own conductor is your only option.

It's time to do some more reflecting. Before moving on, here are a few questions for you to ponder and process:

1. Do you struggle with pride?
2. Has your pride kept you from taking corrective actions to improve yourself and your life?
3. If you knew undoing your pride would essentially help you to reach your best self, would you undo it?

Plane Track

I remember as a kid, I would go downtown with my parents and see the tall buildings. I would go beside the building, and I would look up to them, thinking that they were so gigantic. They seemed endless and as a kid, those buildings seemed so enormous. However, when I became an adult, I began to fly a lot. I would get up in planes that would go 30 and 40 thousand feet in the air. As I sat in my seat and looked out the window, I would look down at the same buildings, and they seemed so small. That was the evidence of my evolution. It was proof that my perspective changed when my position did.

As you grow and as you continuously undo the things that keep you from your best life, you will start to see things differently. Things that were once a big deal become minuscule as you navigate to higher heights in your faith.

Train Track

The last car of a train is a caboose. Caboose means "a house on the deck where the cooking is done." In the past, the train crew would use the roof of the caboose as an observation platform for detecting smoking brakes and other problems. This caboose was also used as a bunkhouse office or kitchen. Technologies like detectors that scan the train's wheels, take temperature readings, and relay information to central locations have rendered the caboose useless.[7]

Things that were once a big deal become minuscule as you navigate to higher heights in your faith.

However, between each car, some cables connect the vehicles together to give it power. The cables maintain a balance of weight between the vehicles, so they don't crash into each

---

7 What was the purpose of the caboose on trains? | Popular Science

other. That is what God does with us, he uses the cable cars of life and connects them to give us power. A funicular (fəˈnɪkjʊlər/) is one of the modes of transportation which uses cable traction for movement on steeply inclined slopes.[8]

According to Popular Science, a funicular railway employs a pair of passenger vehicles that are pulled on a slope by the same cable, which loops over a pulley wheel at the upper end of a track. The vehicles are permanently attached to the ends of the cable and counterbalance each other. They move synchronously: while one vehicle is ascending, the other one is descending the track. These particularities distinguish funiculars from different types of cable railways. For example, a funicular is characterized by an inclined elevator by the presence of two vehicles that counterbalance each other.

Each of the episodes you have gone through in life is the rail car of who you are. The Holy Spirit is the cable that pulls the events together for you and gives you the power you didn't know you had. However, the restoration of your soul through the Holy Spirit develops the ability you have on the inside. Jesus said, "You shall receive power when the Holy Spirit comes upon you. Many think that the power of the Holy Spirit is limited to how he moves during a Sunday morning service, but his power is more. The Holy Spirit gives us the strength to get back on track when life brings us off track.

---

8 What was the purpose of the caboose on trains?

The thing to keep in mind is that restoration can be a detailed and messy process. It is much easier to build a new house than it is to restore one. I like old cars, and to restore one back to the original form is time-consuming and costly. The same is true of houses. When you have an older home or car, it has more character. You have to go to the architect to find out what their original intentions were.

Have you ever been in a house that is being restored? During the restoration, it is dirty and messy, and you have to tear down and scrape and pull the old contents out. You have to tear down everything that everyone else put in the house, five layers of paint, old plumbing, and old electrical wiring. The point is, when you were born, your parents started making you what they wanted you to be. They imparted some wisdom in you, you went to school, and the teachers told you to be quiet and listen, some did things to meet a quota so they could get new gym equipment. The babysitter imparted into you, along with the other people in your environment. Over time without even realizing it, those individuals have placed deposits that have helped shape you into who you into the person you are today. As the master restorer, God wants to strip and pull away all of the layers that cause you to lose your soul and true identity God is trying to help you discover the root of who you are, so you can realize:

1. The power you possess,
2. The gift you have acquired,
3. The anointing that God placed on the inside of you, and

4. The dominion that you walk in.

God will take the messy things in your life that have shaken you to the core to bring you to the point of restoration. During the process of coming out of the mess, your mind will begin to conceptualize that you are more valuable now that God has restored you because when God restores you, you will always come out more powerful than you were before.

"He restoreth my soul." Jesus said, "What does it profit a man to gain the whole world but lose his soul?" The word lose in the Greek translation simply means "what would it profit a man if he gains the respect of a man, but damages his soul in the process." Now according to the hermeneutic, there is a law known as the law of the first dimension. It states that to understand a word or text, you must understand what it meant at the time of the original creation. We must understand how Jesus uses a word at the time, place, setting, tense, etc. We must always remember what God's original intentions for us. Unless we are willing to rely totally and completely on Him, we remain in a place of discontent.

REFLECTION THOUGHT:

Life will demand that we rebuild, reset, and restore often. The whole journey of undoing ordinary involves constant restoration as much as needed. Your challenge is to learn to identify when you need restoration and to partner with God to make it happen.

KEY THREE

Move into Emotional Maturity

OBJECTIVE:

To deal with and challenge your emotional stability. By the end of this step, you will be able to correctly identify what your level of emotional maturity and intelligence is and the steps you can take to make improvements.

"A huge part of spiritual and emotional maturity is recognizing that it's not like you're going to try to fix yourself and become a different person. You remain the same person, but you become awakened."
— Jack Kornfield

If you could pick any song that would serve as the soundtrack of your life, what would that song be? I ask you that because songs have a way of infiltrating the heart and mind without the permission of the person listening to the song. Songs are so powerful in fact that there is an established health profession called music therapy in which music is used to address physical, emotional, cognitive, and social needs of individuals.[1] A song that really touches the heart of a person causes the emotions of that person to rise up, and not just songs that bring up positive emotions. Aggressive songs with aggressive lyrics bring out aggression in people as well. Isn't that interesting? If you're having a hard time conceptualizing this, let me help you. Let's do an exercise. Recite the alphabet. Did you sing the song or hear the tune in your head as you sounded the letters off? That song is responsible for you understanding words, recognizing words, saying words, spelling words, and forming complete sentences. Do you see how powerful songs are? They enter your mind to the point of branching off into more complicated things. These are how your emotions work. They start as one thing and end up going down a spiraling whole if they are not tamed or stewarded well.

Your emotional stability or the lack thereof is what we're going to deal with in this chapter. You owe it to yourself, people in your present, and the people in your future to be emotionally mature and healthy. How you manage your

---

1 American Music Therapy Association

emotions now will lead you to make better decisions in your relationships, your work, and even your walk with God. Our feelings can be very fleeting, we must have the rule over them instead of them having control over us. It is essential to train yourself to understand that you are more powerful than your emotions are. In fact, your emotions only have the power that you give them.

When our emotions are what we use to make decisions or steer our lives, we risk living a very inconsistent lifestyle that is comprised of a lot of thoughtless actions. We decide on things impulsively and do things without filtering our actions accordingly. Untamed emotions can lead to inconsistency in your decision making concerning your money, time, and even what you allow for entertaining you. These and many other things can all be affected by our emotions if we're not mindful of pursuing an emotionally healthy life. As I mentioned earlier, emotions can spiral into other complexities, leaving us dumbfounded in the process of living the extraordinary life that God desires us to have.

It's Ok To Be Emotional

Please, don't misunderstand me. I am not saying that there is anything wrong with having emotions or being emotional. It is absolutely okay to be emotional and have cognition of your feelings. Even Jesus had emotions. There are two accounts in the Bible, which show us that Jesus had emotional moments.

"When he looked out over the crowds, his heart broke."
(Matthew 9:36 MSG)

"Jesus wept." **(John 11:35)**

If you find that dealing with your emotions is something you're challenged by because you were taught that being emotional is a sign of weakness, you might have to undo that mentality. The first step to undoing an unhealthy mindset is to attain the proper mindset concerning something. That is to say, you must find out the truth about your emotions. What are they? Why do they exist? How can you control and deal with them?

We live in a world that has conditioned men and women to suppress their feelings. Men are told that they need to be tough and can't show emotion. Women are told that they are too emotional. But the human species would walk around like a bunch of zombies if it were not for emotions. In a lot of ways, that's how many people

Your emotions fuel your thoughts, and your thoughts create your world.

function in their daily lives, like a zombie. This is not how it should be. This is not what God intended for humanity whatsoever. God made us emotional beings.

Emotions are what God uses to bring awareness to events and happenings in our lives. Without knowing how we feel about certain things, it makes it hard for us to balance and give proper language and identity to our thoughts. Even if we don't know what to think, we can undoubtedly describe how we feel. And as a result of understanding how we feel, we can begin to formulate thoughts. Your emotions fuel your thoughts, and your thoughts create your world.

"He that is faithful in a very little is faithful also in much: and he that is unrighteous in a very little is unrighteous also in much." **(Luke 16:10)**

Just about every single time the above scripture is mentioned, the topic of money is what is discussed, but I would like to offer you a different perspective. Money isn't the only thing we should be faithful with. Yes, it is a significant part of our lives, and according to the Word of God, money provides answers, but faithfulness extends far beyond the monetary aspect of our lives. We also have to be faithful in our emotional health, being intentional about how we posture ourselves to handle life's highs and lows. We tend to make some not so wise decisions when our emotions are in the driver's seat. Here are a few examples.

Anger

What is the first thing you do when someone makes you angry? Do you immediately fly off the handle and let them know how you feel? Or do you quickly retreat and drawback into a shell avoiding the person, situation, and argument?

You can be honest here. There's no right or wrong answer, and nobody is around to judge you. This is about self-reflection and using the power of awareness to identify your pattern. Emotional triggers are people, words, opinions, situations, or environmental situations that provoke an intense and excessive emotional reaction within us. We all have triggers, but we must take responsibility for our own actions. Placing the blame or responsibility on someone else is giving them more power than they're meant to have. That is the key. Anger is a natural emotion. Ephesians 4:26-27 says, "Be angry but do not sin, do not let the sun go down on your anger and do not make room for the devil." This reminds us that although being angry is a natural emotion, what we do when we're mad can give the enemy an access point into our lives if we're not careful. What you do when you're angry also determines your emotional intelligence.

In the article, *Why Emotional Intelligence is crucial for success*, emotional intelligence is described as the "capacity of being aware of, in control of, expressing one's emotions, and handling interpersonal relationships judiciously and empathetically."[2] Every action and reaction is your responsibility—and no one else's, despite what they might have done to you. Want to express your anger concerning something fully? That's absolutely acceptable, but you must be ready to own that.

---

2 Why Emotional Intelligence Is Crucial for Success (Entrepreneur.com)

Being a Hot Head

If you fall into the category of immediately flying off the handle, this is what we're going to use to define that characteristic. This doesn't mean that you're labeling yourself. We're just making distinctions.

Not much thought goes into the response of the person who immediately cracks the whip to let the person that angered them know how they are feeling. The danger in this is that when a person is angry, all of the negative things they think about themselves and the person that they are upset with rise to the surface. And because those thoughts are very rarely expressed when they aren't angry, they fester and become toxic to the person holding them in. Those thoughts have not been stewarded well. At the moment of anger, those things come out in the form of words and sometimes actions that a person cannot take back. You see, even your thought life is connected to your emotions. When you don't have a healthy emotional life, you react to things that offend you instead of adequately responding to them. Billy Graham was once quoted as saying, "Hot Heads and cold hearts never solve anything."

Turtle Turtle

If you are the person who retreats and avoids conflict, we are going to identify that characteristic as you hiding in a shell. This is also dangerous because you probably think a lot without saying much of anything. Those thoughts left unexpressed also begin to fester and intoxicate your life, and all that is associated with it. You might even start to respond to others in a way that you are not aware of. Your power and will to relationally resolve how you feel is stunted, preventing you from growing in relationships or understanding the person you're angry with.

Most people who drawback and retreat, when they are angry, are most times passive-aggressive. What this means is that they'll do certain things without being direct about them, leaving those actions up for wrong interpretation and even miscommunication. On the other hand, you must be willing to address anything that happened years ago. You shouldn't worry about letdowns or things of that nature. When I use the term 'letdown,' you may proceed with the assumption that this is a continuation of something that happened in the past. I have decided to use it as an opportunity to address and see it as a situational disappointment. It is a temporary situation and should not be viewed as a permanent state.

The Remedy

There are several things you can do to deal with your anger in a healthy way. Step back for a moment and collect your thoughts before you speak, and give yourself a time limit on how long you are willing to let the situation remain in your thoughts. Frequently, we forget that we have the final say in what controls us and what we allow to breach our barrier of peace. Creating a barrier of peace in your life means that you draw a line in the sand in regards to the situations and people you allow to impact you negatively. Although you can't control what comes to you, you can certainly control what stays with you. You don't have to journey through life with unhealthy and toxic attachments that erode and decay your quality of life.

Having someone you trust to express how you feel about a situation is always healthy. This goes back to the Relational Agreement piece you read earlier. It can be a great help to you if you let it. Finally, your relationship with God has to come into play at some point. It should be your first response to anger. It won't always be the case, but casting your cares on Him should be in the mix somewhere, somehow. Prayer and worship are what God uses to make us stable.[3] In prayer and in worship lies the answers that God wants to give us. Especially when He calls us into a new thing. He does away with the things of our past and settles our thoughts and emotions by giving us insight as to how we can become better stewards over our emotions.[4]

Excitement

There are moments of joy that lift us up or get our adrenaline going. And enthusiasm is excellent, but even in our excitement, we can still make bad decisions. More often than not, we aren't considering the possible outcomes of a

---

3 1 Samuel 16:14:23
4 1 Samuel 9

thing when we're excited. The only thing flooding our minds is what's happening at the moment. All of the chemical reactions that we have in a moment of excitement don't leave us with much room to have any rational thoughts or make any rational decisions.

The Impulse Buyer

Without going beyond the thought of "oh, that looks really nice, and it's on sale," this personality type has tunnel vision when it comes to exciting things or moments that bring them pleasure. Again, the end result of things is rarely considered until a much later time. The risk of being impulsive is that the unpleasant outcome is sometimes only considered when that outcome has occurred. At that moment, a person has to shift back into survival mode. This happens when a person tries to recover from an unpleasant result prompted by an unwise decision made in a moment of excitement.

The Indecision Maker

In moments of excitement, some people clam up or become very paranoid at any moment that might seem too good to be true. Excitement thrusts someone with this personality type into indecision. They make the decision to not make any decisions out of fear of making the wrong decision. This is oxymoronic because indecision often hinders people's life, leaving outcomes that they can control to just mere happenstance. This is a perilous way to live life.

What is the Remedy?

"For God gave us not a spirit of fearfulness; but of power and love and discipline." **(2 Timothy 1:7 ASV)**

Even during moments of excitement, we should lean on God for direction. There's still a life to live afterward and the right decisions to make. This is all a part of balancing out your emotions so that you respond to life in emotional maturity. That is the point of this chapter, sparking thoughts and strategies in you that prompt you to pursue emotional maturity, a maturity that drives and has dominion over emotions that can be one in one state today and another tomorrow. You'll find that as you pursue emotional health, you'll learn to properly manage other areas of your life because life has the propensity to take us on a roller coaster ride of emotions.

When reviewing these emotions, how have they impeded your growth? Have you found that your behaviors have kept you from reaching your potential? What do you think God is trying to share with you in these moments of emotional weakness? It's not enough to announce that your emotions may drive you to act in a particular manner. Once you recognize the emotion and the impact it has on your outward and inward being, it is crucial to make the necessary adjustment in our response. This is growth, this is undoing ordinary.

EXERCISE:

Everyone has at least one toxic emotional trait. Maybe it's being passive-aggressive. Identify your trait, dedicate intentional time to undo it, and replace it with a better trait.

List your trait here: _____.

KEY FOUR

Move from Hurt to Spiritual Alertness

OBJECTIVE:

To encourage you to be effective at managing your emotions versus being an emotional hoarder; and to prompt you to release hurt in order to forgive and to live a life that is spiritually pleasing to God.

"I am just an ordinary person committed to doing extraordinary things."
— Iyanla Vanzant

"Love endures long and is patient and kind; love never is envious nor boils over with jealousy, is not boastful or vainglorious, does not display itself haughtily. [5] It is not conceited (arrogant and inflated with pride); it is not rude (unmannerly) and does not act unbecomingly. Love (God's love in us) does not insist on its own rights or its own way, for it is not self-seeking; it is not touchy or fretful or resentful; it takes no account of the evil done to it. It pays no attention to a suffered wrong. [6] It does not rejoice at injustice and unrighteousness, but rejoices when right and truth prevail. [7] Love bears up under anything and everything that comes, is ever ready to believe the best of every person, its hopes are fadeless under all circumstances, and it endures everything without weakening." **(1 Corinthians 13:4-7 AMPC)**

Before we dive in, here are some focus questions for you:
1. How good are you at loving people?
2. How good are you at letting go?
3. Would you say that your emotions have taken rule over you?

Let's take a moment to sit and think about what our lives would be like if God held on to everything that we do that does not please Him. It sounds like a daunting task to endure, right? If we would carefully consider how relentlessly God pursues us in love, we would see how awful it would be if He did the same concerning our shortcomings. It is an understatement to say that we wouldn't have a life at all. But in His infinite grace and love, God is patient with us and kind to us when it comes to our destiny.

He knows that we are going to make mistakes and that we aren't going to get everything right. He knows that it is going to take multiple efforts for us to be the best version of ourselves, the version God had in mind when He created us. The God who knows everything about us isn't surprised at our mistakes. Disappointed? Perhaps. Surprised? Not even a little bit. He is too sovereign and all-knowing to be caught by surprise. He's not even surprised by our successes and all of the things we do right. This is the character of God. He honors His children, and He knows them quite well, better than they know themselves.

> For many of us, our emotions have become idols. They've gotten in the way of God staying in the center of our lives.

I just gave you insight into the way that God desires for you to see Him. My aim in doing that is to push you towards consciously living in the freedom of knowing that God's love towards you knows no limits. If you do not grab hold of that reality and let it settle in your heart, what we are about to discuss next, won't mean anything to you, neither will it work for you. Once you grab ahold of the depths of God's all-encompassing love, you will be able to experience the abundant life he died for you to have.

The Burden of Holding On

For many of us, our emotions have become idols. They've gotten in the way of God staying in the center of our lives.

All of us, at some point, have allowed our emotions to steer our decision making. Whether it comes to people we love, places we go, or things we acquire, how we manage our relationships with them are sometimes done in the error of our emotions. And because some of us are emotional hoarders, we, consciously and subconsciously, overload ourselves with the cares of this world and everyday life. What a load to bear!

Emotions are very potent. They are catalysts to the actions we portray to others. However, emotional hoarding is even more powerful. Emotion hoarding could be something that people aren't aware of, or maybe it's something that they are aware of, but they just don't give it much attention. Most people emotionally hoard because they don't want to deal with or confront specific issues with others. If something hurts us or makes us feel great, we hold on to the thought of that person, place, or thing, sometimes, longer than we should. Occasionally, we even get to the point of those things becoming an idol in our hearts. An idol is anything that we've primarily made bigger than God in our lives. It's the people, places, and things that occupy the throne of our heart—a space that is ultimately meant for God, and Him alone, to fill.

Whenever things become idols, our minds are in a place where we can mistake the feelings and thoughts we have as God's activity in our lives, when what we're really experiencing is the consequence of depending on our own thoughts and feelings to guide us through life. Good feelings, bad feelings, excellent outcomes, and horrible outcomes can all become things that replace God's lordship over our lives.

One of the things we tend to hoard the most is what someone has negatively done to us. The hoarding of emotions and thoughts from an offense done against you morphs into one of the vilest things that a person can have in their heart - unforgiveness. It seems to literally chain the soul of a person to the flaws and mistakes of the person who offended them. Most people don't think of unforgiveness in these terms. What is typically focused on when it comes to unforgiveness is what the offender has done. But that is not at all that unforgiveness is. The offense is just that, a habit, a mistake, or a flaw a person has.

Don't allow yourself to be controlled by unforgiveness. It is also the direct opposite of the character of God and the character He desires for you to have. Unforgiveness is a form of idolatry. You may ask how can emotions towards people become idols. When you choose to have bitterness towards someone, you have given that person the authority to change your mood at any time of the day. That person doesn't have to be present, the mere hearing of his/her name could ultimately rouse strong emotions and outbursts, and eventually lead to you having a bad day. You may be walking down the street, but because you see that person walking in the same direction, you change your route. You may be going for a networking event, but because you hear that person's voice, you turn around. You may say to yourself, "I'd rather die than be in the same room as _____ or breathe the same air they are breathing."

Unforgiveness is the worship of offense or the emotions and thoughts you have regarding an offense. It is a form of idolatry. As a result, you've disobeyed the number one commandment that God gave to His people in the Old and New testaments; you've worshiped another god and have deliberately chosen not to love your neighbor. Do you see how deep unforgiveness runs? It's much more complex and entangled than the simplicity of what someone said or did to you.

Unforgiveness comes with so many consequences. It can lead to loss of control of emotions. I have seen people who have lost loved ones because they chose to keep their anger or resentment towards them. It can lead to unnecessary high blood pressure and increased heart rate. Sometimes, unforgiveness can lead to severe depression, anxiety, post-traumatic stress disorders, and high levels of stress. The emotional pain you feel is almost commensurate to the pain you get from a physical injury. You may not realize this, but unforgiveness drastically affects your health.

There are many causes of unforgiveness, but I'll only mention a few critical ones:

1. Pride

A leading cause of unforgiveness is pride. This is evident when you have a high opinion of yourself, and look down on others or make others feel like they don't matter. It can come in the form of you not wanting to show any type of weakness or vulnerability towards someone. In society, there is even a misconception that vulnerability is only for the weak and low-hearted. People would go to lengths to make sure they appear as more powerful in any given situation. I've seen pride destroy marriages. People who were, once, in love and happily married got divorced because one spouse was too proud to say, "I'm sorry" or own up to their mistakes.

2. Bitterness

Bitterness is the bi-product of unforgiveness. Sometimes we carry bitterness in our hearts because of how someone has wronged us. Perhaps, the person who committed the offense never apologized. As a result, over time roots of bitterness develop in your heart and can stifle your ability to display love to those around you. Bitterness if left unaddressed, can cause you to destroy God ordained friendships or relationships because a bitter person sees everything through a negative sense. Don't allow bitterness to stop you from receiving the blessings God has for you on the other side of your pain. Remember, no matter how badly someone has hurt you, the decision to move forward towards healing is your choice, not theirs.

3. Hatred

Hate is a powerful word. It means you absolutely detest someone, and you wish the worst thing in life for them. The scriptures say if you have a problem with your brother, "In your anger, do not sin: do not let the sun go down while you are still angry, and do not give the devil a foothold.[1] If you give the devil a foothold, it could easily turn to a stronghold. You start to wonder how a little argument with your spouse led to a shoulder dislocation or a

"You can't control other people. You can only control your reactions to them."

-Anonymous

miscarriage. Even an argument towards a loved one could turn to resentment. I've seen fathers against sons, mothers against daughters, husbands against wives, sisters against sisters and brothers against brothers. Don't give the enemy room to sow seeds of resentment, make the right choice. There's a famous quote that says, "You can't control other people. You can only control your reactions to them."

When you choose to forgive others, you free yourself from all emotional strains. You walk around with a lightness in your spirit. Being the first to say, 'I'm sorry' or 'I forgive you' is not a sign of weakness; it's a sign of strength. It shows that you are aware of your identity in Christ. You know who you are. If you know who you are in Christ and

---

1 Ephesians 4:26, NIV

you genuinely believe it, you wouldn't even have the time to find offense in people. For instance, if my co-worker makes negative comments or spreads terrible rumors, I wouldn't find offense because I know whatever they say is not a true reflection of who I am. I am who God says I am. He says I am the head and not the tail. He says I am heir to His throne. Since I dwell in His presence, I abide under His shadow. He says I am a blessing to nations. I AM A CHOSEN PEOPLE. I AM A ROYAL PRIESTHOOD. I AM A CHOSEN GENERATION. Always remember, what God said about you will always outweigh the opinions of those around you.

This is why it is crucial to have the mind of Christ. Once you have the mind of Christ, trivial gossip will not affect you. At the end of the day, we are running this race called life. Life is filled with many obstacles. Will you choose to let the little barriers keep you down or run like a hurdler and jump every hurdle? Life is too short to hold grudges. Life is too short to hold onto negative emotional baggage.

The foundation and premise of your Christian walk should be the love of God.

One way to remove emotional baggage is to resolve issues as soon as you can. Hoarding emotions can be very detrimental to your mental health. Sometimes, you can have these conversations or situations replay in your mind. You wish you had given that co-worker or supervisor a piece of your mind.

95

You wish your ex got hit by a truck, so she feels the same pain you felt when she left you for another man. No one needs a piece of your mind, choose to show a piece of God's thoughts towards them. This may prove difficult, but it is this love that separates us from others.

In the scriptures, the Pharisees wanted to use the law to test Jesus. They asked him, "Teacher, which is the greatest commandment in the Law?" He responded, "Love the Lord your God with all your heart and with all your soul and with all your mind... Love your neighbor as yourself."[2] If you want to please God, love others as you would love yourself. Go the extra mile.

When you choose to walk in love despite how someone has wronged you, you are choosing to walk from your place of pain towards healing.

The foundation and premise of your Christian walk should be the love of God. Every step you take should be taken in love. Every word you speak should be said in love. Every relationship you have should be stewarded in love. Love conquers all.

When it comes to unforgiveness, love has no influence on the heart because it has no influence on the mind. Love is a well thought out choice. The love of God is unconditional and gives us an opportunity to choose him.

---

2 Matthew 22:37-39, NIV

Can you honestly say that when someone offends you, the first thing that comes to your mind is how much you love them or how much you would choose to think highly of them? Probably not. That is exactly what God does when we go against His will. He doesn't submit Himself to our will and choose not to forgive or love us, He continues to operate by His will. We should imitate this behavior. We should live according to His will, His love, and His desires. That is how you make sure that you move on from past hurts and betrayals that you are allowing to affect your present and construct a destructive future for yourself. When you choose to walk in love despite how someone has wronged you, you are choosing to walk from your place of pain towards healing.

Mercy Makes It Easier

"Love bears up under anything and everything that comes, is ever ready to believe the best of every person, its hopes are fadeless under all circumstances, and it endures everything without weakening." **(1 Corinthians 13:7 AMPC)**

Many people wish for a more comfortable life and also pursue an easy life. Without realizing it, they go on this pursuit in ways that only add more difficulty to their lives. Most times, their efforts and intentions are good, but what they have failed to do is consider how their relationships affect the function and prosperity of their everyday lives. The lives of people who seek an easier path through life don't typically have a keen understanding of patience with themselves and other people. If they took the time to assess the quality and longevity of their relationships, they would find that their life has become a revolving door of sorts. They've either been dropped or have dropped others due to a lack of patience and kindness, and the mercy that God so freely gives to them, they refuse to exemplify to those around them I willingly admit that it is not always easy to extend mercy, but when it is extended it makes your life easier to manage because loving-kindness makes your relationships better. When your relationships operate by compassion, and you engage with people based on who they are when you think the best of them, you get the best out of them, and the best comes out of you. This is the way you lighten the load of the burden you carry in life.

This is how you display the character of God. In His mercy, He shows you, people that are hurting as much as you are, they're broken just like you are, and they need compassion as much as you do. So if you need it and you know they need it, extend mercy, and it will be given to you. That simple right? Easy to say and can be very difficult to do, but with the help of God, it's more than achievable. You can excel in mercy and make your life easier!

REFLECTION QUESTIONS:

1. What's one way you plan to put mercy into action in your everyday life?

2. Who are the people that you have trouble forgiving that you need to extend mercy towards?

KEY FIVE

Step into the Flow

OBJECTIVE:

To expand your understanding of the practical application of love-inspired decision making in solving problems in your world and walking in God's divine wisdom.

"There is no fear in love dread does not exist, but full-grown (complete, perfect) love turns fear out of doors and expels every trace of terror! For fear brings with it the thought of punishment, and so he who is afraid has not reached the full maturity of love is not yet grown into love's complete perfection." **(1 John 4:18 AMPC)**

Without understanding, there are many things in life that most people won't try to do unless they're just a thrill seeker or risk-taker. And even those types of people have limits to what they will do. People don't typically move beyond their understanding or beyond their knowledge of a thing. You might have those that answer questions they have no language for or have any idea as to what they are talking about, but they will make it seem as if they have all of the answers.

The error in moving beyond your understanding or scope of knowledge is that it's pretty challenging to consider the cost or to consider the end result of a thing. At the root of all actions committed beyond a person's understanding, is a lack of desire to make informed decisions. For the risk-takers that move beyond knowledge, if you have all of the questions answered, you're still taking a risk because there's no guarantee that the outcome of a thing will come out as intended. So why not go ahead and get as much information as you can? At the end of the day, it's still a risk, right? If, for whatever reason, you always seem to be doing things without the proper understanding and knowledge, that's a habit you need to undo. Your norm should never be moving throughout life without being armed with adequate knowledge of how things work.

Wisdom is profitable to whoever receives, and if you are in need of wisdom, ask God (James 1:5). Some things are not found in the hands of man but the hands of God. There are many battles you wouldn't have had to fight if you had the wisdom to tackle the issue at hand. In the scriptures, out of all the many things Solomon could have asked for, he simply asked for more wisdom. Think of the time, he would have spent trying to solve all of the problems that came his way, if he didn't have wisdom, he could have fought battles that he was not equipped to handle.

In our modern-day, the wealthiest and most powerful people are those who used their wisdom to solve worldwide problems. This information has become the thing that nations crave for. Countries have felt the impact of people applying their knowledge to make the world a better place. People like Mark Zuckerberg and Bill Gates come to mind. They have used wisdom to build an empire for themselves. They have used this same wisdom to produce substantial resources, fund just causes, and tackle impossible tasks.

Movement matters.

For example, the Bill Gates' foundation has invested so much in HIV/AIDS prevention and cure. You probably have the same capacity to solve huge problems but haven't come to the realization that you can solve substantial problems. Everyone is looking for that person that can make their life a little better. Choose to be that person. You are the solution that someone is looking for.

When you are prepared to do something, and you have the right information, there's a specific flow that you develop while accomplishing that task. God even said that there is a time for action, which is what we see with Moses. In Exodus

14, verse 15, Pharaoh's army was closing in on the people of Israel, and Moses was in prayer. God spoke to Moses and asked why he was crying out to him and told him to get the children of Israel moving. Once God speaks, it is time to move.

QUESTION:

How quickly do you move once you've been equipped to do a thing?

Whether you are developing a relationship, growing a business, or working in ministry, having a flow is necessary. Movement matters. It is crucial. There must be something you funnel all of your activity through. There must be a conduit, and that conduit is God's love. Love should be the foundation of all that we do, because love is an informed decision. Love is a choice— sometimes made without all the details but a choice,

Love should be the conduit of the entirety of your life.

nonetheless. Choosing to love and to do things in love means that we carefully and considerately think things through before we put our hands to them.

One thing that I want to reiterate is that we have lived our lives as if love is just an emotion or a feeling that is produced in us, but that is far from the truth. Love produces emotions, but it first starts in the mind; it is how you approach people, places, and things. Love should be the conduit of the entirety of your life. Everything should flow through the filter of love.

Earlier in this chapter, we discussed people not moving beyond what they know. Now, I want to put some reason to that so you can think through why you may not be doing what you should be doing, or why you are not currently where you should be.

Merriam Webster states that a conduit, in esoteric, and spiritual discourse, is a specific object, person, location, or process (such as engaging in a séance or entering a trance) which allows a person to connect or communicate with a spiritual realm, metaphysical energy, or spiritual entity, or vice versa.

What are you a conduit of, and what do people receive from your presence? What are you walking in? You must be a conduit so people can see Christ in a form they have never seen before. The conduits of grace and mercy are the very distributors of love.

Therefore, be careful in judging people and their situations. You can only remove the plank in your eye, which will take you a lifetime. Judging is the trick of the devil to occupy the time you need to not only be praying for them but also loving them. Sometimes, circumstances and environments shape people.

You may judge someone, but you haven't lived their life or experienced their experiences. You may have grown up in a perfect neighborhood with an ideal family. The person you are judging may have had the exact opposite in life. Always ask God to give you the wisdom to see people the way he sees them.

We need to love without walls and forgive without contingency barriers.

It's a mighty prayer. When you see people the way God sees them, it wouldn't be hard for you to love them. You will see the hidden treasures in that person that society has buried with condemnation.

We must love others and excuse the inexcusable because God has forgiven the inexcusable in us. We must learn to love without walls and forgive without contingency barriers. If someone falls into sin, forgivingly restore that person, saving your critical comments for yourself. You might be needing forgiveness yourself, before the day is out. Reach out and intentionally love those who are oppressed. This is love in action. This is what God expects from us. If you think you are too good for that, you are deceived and are holding up your blessings by focusing on yourself. Therefore, love others unconditionally for you to grow yourself as a conduit of Christ.[1]

Fear & Lethargy

What you don't know is and always will be a barrier in between you and the future that God has for you. God is so interested in you knowing what you need to know that He makes His thoughts available to you. He is full of great mysteries, His ways that are not like ours, and thoughts that are not like ours, but yet, everything He knows and all that is hidden in Him, He still makes His thoughts available to us. We just have to have the mindset to actively seek Him for what we need to know.

It is also worth mentioning that God is willing and ready to supply the wisdom that you need for your life. The Bible states in James 1:5 that if any of you lack wisdom, ask of God. There is access to boundless wisdom when you stop relying on your limited knowledge and rely on God. He wants to give it to you freely. And if you're going to undo ordinary successfully, you're going to need to get into the habit of asking for wisdom frequently and intentionally.

Often times, the thing that keeps us from operating in this divine knowledge is fear. Think about that for a moment. At the beginning of this chapter, I quoted 1 John 4:18. My reason for doing that is so that we could come to this very point. Many people think that the opposite of fear is faith, but if you search God's word, faith and fear are not mentioned together or in opposition to each other. In fact, two passages of scripture show fear and love in opposition to one another. The scripture referenced above says, "perfect love casts out fear," and in 2 Timothy 1:7, it says, "God has not given us the spirit of fear, but of power, of love, and of a sound mind." If we work backward through that scripture, we're going to hit something that proves just how much our minds have to do with love.

To be of a sound mind means that you respond intelligently to people and situations. I already mentioned that love is a decision. What I haven't mentioned, however, is the word 'power.' In this scripture, that word means ability. Then, we get to the word 'fear.' To have fear means that you are letting your life be governed by irrational thoughts. What you can do is often overshadowed by the thought of what you can't do. More often than not, what you can't do has absolutely nothing to do with the situation at hand. Fear will bring up outcomes that are not worthy of mentioning, as well as outcomes that will talk you out of doing something that you should actually do. Is this relatable to you?

Since love is an informed decision, and it drives out fear, it further proves that fear is the enemy of love and not the enemy of faith. When you are moving in fear, a sound mind is impossible to possess, because of irrational thinking. Sound mindedness is intelligent thinking or disciplined thinking that gives you consistency in a thing so that you can progress forward.

Fear seemingly cements your feet in a place where you feel

as if you cannot move beyond where you are. When you are in this space of feeling stuck, you've probably entered into an unhealthy cycle that comes along with frustration. And the more frustrated a person's mind becomes, the more tired their body becomes, and this leads to lethargy or a cycle of just being tired all the time. The remedy for this is doing everything that you do in love. A doctor once said, "The best medicine for humans is love." Someone asked, "What if it doesn't work?" He smiled and said, "Increase the dosage."

Becoming Love

Because God commands us to live our lives in the likeness and image of him, we should strive to exemplify His character. Since God is love[2], we should love, too. We should ask ourselves this question daily, how can I be a living walking breathing example of God's love on earth to those around me? The way we can achieve this is to simply ask Him to teach us to love others by first teaching us to love Him selflessly. As a byproduct of learning to love God, we end up doing everything else in His love, subsequently becoming His love. This is how you become a conduit. When you stop loving from a selfish place, love begins to flow through you, and everything that you do is done from a foundation of love.

Love is so powerful. It can make you do extraordinary things.

---

2 1 John 4:8

I have heard a lot of people say love is blind and I couldn't agree more. Love sees no wrong. Have you ever seen a man who falls in love? You probably have, seeing as there are so many generic romantic movies out there. A man's desire for a woman would make him do crazy things. He would buy her the best dresses, take her to the most expensive restaurants, and take her to the most exotic places in the world.

Remember this, you can only give what you have. I receive love; therefore, I give love. If you try to give love when you have no love, you would be running on a deficit. You may appear jovial around others but struggle with depression behind closed doors. There is a love that knows no bounds, and that is the love Christ offers to us. I can

Always remember that you, too, are worthy of the same love that you give to others.

love people because Jesus Christ loved me first. So, when I converse with people, I don't operate from a place of hurt. I love with an understanding.

Make it a daily action to seek God's love every day. When you do this, it would be so hard to get angry when someone steps on your toes. Trivial issues wouldn't push you to act out of love.

While loving others, you must also remember to love yourself. Always remember that you, too, are worthy of the same love that you give to others. Know your worth.

When you know your worth, there are certain things that you wouldn't tolerate from people. You won't allow people talk you down or insult you. You won't let people's words or actions get to you. You may do things that disappoint your Heavenly Father, but NO SIN can separate you from HIS LOVE. Not even the hatred you feel towards yourself can stop God's love from penetrating into the deepest, darkest crevices of your heart.

The person that seeks righteousness will always discover love because God is love. When you seek God, you will always discover the truth. To put it in the words of St. Augustine: to fall in love with God is the greatest romance; to seek him is the greatest adventure; to find him, is the greatest human achievement.

REFLECTION QUESTIONS:

1. What's the biggest challenge you have with flowing in love?
2. Have you encountered a traumatic experience that makes it challenging to love freely?
3. What are 3 proactive ways that you can reflect the love of God to those around you?

Drop your Anchor

OBJECTIVE:

Discover the unstoppable power resident in placing our faith in the unmovable, unstoppable force of God's love and faithfulness when faced with the burdens and cares of life.

"A hero is an ordinary person doing things in an extraordinary way."
— Christopher Reeve

Weight is something that affects our lives in many different ways. Sometimes, it harms us, and other times it helps. In this chapter, we're going to talk about both. Some people are often not aware of the weight that they carry. This can prove to be a detriment to themselves and everyone around them.

In some cases, they don't give the very best of themselves to others. Consequently, others don't receive the very best of that person even though it's something they may need. This is how relationships end up becoming corrupt and becoming pieces of baggage that people carry around.

A relationship that starts out great, but loses its luster after a while, for whatever reason, is the most common bad weight that people experience in their lives. I believe that the reason behind this is the relationship and network that exists in the Kingdom. Any enemy of God's Kingdom would have it that all of our relationships become hindrances, and this is why we need to wake up. It only takes one of your relationships to deteriorate for the trajectory of your life to take a wrong turn. That is how powerful relationships are.

Relationships govern everything that we do. Even if we don't belong to the Kingdom, relationships govern our lives in some way or another. Relationships can build us or tear us down. They can make us hopeful or hopeless. Relationships either weigh us down or lift us up. Relationships anchor us or cause us to float away. Someone once said that "relationship is the currency of the Kingdom," and they were absolutely correct. Relationships are the most powerful resource that the Kingdom of God and the Kingdom of hell have. They matter so much to God that he was very clear in scripture when He stated that it's not good for man to dwell alone. [1]

---

1 Genesis 2:18

It is God's plan to see all mankind in relationship with each other.

The Cycle You Didn't See Coming

There is a different type of weight that doesn't have to affect us negatively. This particular weight might not always be comfortable, but it definitely benefits us. The weight I'm referring to is the kind that exercises the parts of us that we usually ignore or the parts of us that we pridefully think are perfect until we meet a barrier that puts pressure on us. It is what we experience when we feel we have it all figured out, but the pressure reveals our imperfections.

One thing that we should all aspire to do is grow beyond what we think we have mastered because it's after you've stepped outside of your comfort zone that you begin to change, grow, and transform. If we can prevent ourselves from plateauing, we can prevent ourselves from falling into cycles. Cycles end up becoming a bad weight and end up causing instability in every area of your life. Those cycles result in soul issues, bringing about instability in the mind, will, and emotions.

If you can't tell already, we're about to discuss the inner workings of the soul further. I press on matters of the soul because of how they affect the life and quality of our Christian walk. When we confessed our belief in the death, burial, and resurrection of Jesus Christ as Lord of all, our souls were saved. But, that did not mean that everything concerning our soul was repaired in that moment of confession. This is because we still have a life to live after our confession, there's still some undoing and unraveling of things wrapped around our souls that we have to address and correct.

Soul work is a lifelong process that consists of levels, stages, and phases of healing. Within this process, there are progressions and even regressions. There are ups and downs.

Experience without theory is blind, but theory without experience is mere intellectual play.[2] God takes us through life's amusement park as a greater testament to His Glory. To imply one walks with God but shows no morsel of internal faith nor repentance is a discreet way of insulting God's intelligence. Like any other part of life, there are negatives, positives, and in-betweens. The healing of the soul takes time and a lot of intention. It takes the support of friends, close friends, mentors, and accountability partners. Most importantly, it takes total submission to God, the captain of your soul.

The Captain of Your Soul

What guides your soul the most? Where do you go for answers in your life? Is it your friends, family, social media, your zodiac sign or horoscope? Who and/or what is the Lord of your decision making? Your decision making has a

2 Immanuel Kant Quotes - BrainyQuote

lord. It is the thing or things that hold the greatest weight of influence in your decision making. Take a moment to really reflect on that. The truth of the matter is that we all submit ourselves to something or someone. From the moment we are conceived, we submit and depend on something or someone to live. This does not mean we're always aware of who or what we're submitted to, but we submit regardless.

Now, after really taking the time to think about that, if you're submitted to God, then you're in good hands. If it's not God, then there's still good news, because He still wants to be the One you're submitted to. You would just need to commit to making whatever changes are necessary to ensure that God, and He alone, is Lord over your entire life, especially your decision making. Whether you know it or not, or fully understand, God truly wants to be the One who you have let be the Lord of your life. God wants to be the Captain of your soul.

He wants you to be in a ship where the Holy Spirit is the steering wheel so that you don't take control of things using your own strength. He wants to use the winds and waves that He commands to steer and push you toward the places He wants you to be. If you read the story of Noah in Genesis, you'll notice that all of the specific instructions that God gave to Noah, He never made mention of a steering wheel. He instructed Noah with specific measurements of the ark. He even told him to put a window in it, but nothing to control the ark was installed.

I believe that this is how God wants us to live our lives with Him in total control. He intends to be the captain your ship, your life, and your soul.

One of my favorite poems is Invictus by William Earnest Henley:

Out of the night that covers me,
Black as the Pit from pole to pole,
I thank whatever gods may be
For my unconquerable soul.

In the fell clutch of circumstance
I have not winced nor cried aloud.
Under the bludgeonings of chance
My head is bloody, but unbowed.

Beyond this place of wrath and tears
Looms but the Horror of the shade,
And yet the menace of the years
Finds, and shall find me unafraid.

It matters not how strait the gate,
How charged with punishments the scroll.
I am the master of my fate:
I am the captain of my soul.

– William Ernest Henley

How Storms Benefit You

Can we first agree that storms are beneficial? Sure, they are not the most ideal things to experience, and no one is waking up in the morning, thinking, "I wonder what storms I can get into today." However, storms will come, and when they do, we must understand that, depending on our perspective and mentality, they can do us a lot of good.

A while back, I learned a nautical term that blew me away when I started to realize how much my life with God resembled it. That term is 'kedging.' It means to throw the anchor of your ship into the water during a storm. It's when you toss your anchor towards the storm. During a storm out at sea, the wind and the waves can be hazardous. What kedging does is it puts the extra weight at the bottom of a ship to stabilize it while the tides are violently raging against it. In my personal life, I've experienced storms that I now look back on and realize that it was for my good.

I remember the time I went to pick up my daughter from my ex-wife's residence during her birthday weekend. I picked her up at a party that my ex-wife threw for her. She had a few of her friends over. I was excited to pick her up because I planned to give my daughter a surprise party near my home. I had people waiting to surprise her at another party, and they were anxiously awaiting her arrival.

While picking her up, an argument ensued between my ex,

her family, and myself. In her effort to sabotage my good intentions, the police were called, and I was taken to jail. To make matters worse, this was on a Saturday, so the judge wasn't going to hear cases until Monday morning. I went to jail at about 3:00pm that afternoon and went through the process of being booked, and was kept in a holding cell until 4:00am the next morning. I got to my cell, and a gentleman was on the bottom bunk, sitting up, praying. He immediately said to me, "Hi, my name is Collins, and God told me you were coming." I explained to him that I was exhausted, frustrated, and was not really up for any talking to anyone because I didn't want to be here.

Collins goes on to say that God told him my name was Rico and that he brought me here for a reason. I was amazed that he knew my name, and I told him I just wanted to get some rest. I was a bit skeptical and thought that perhaps, he saw my name on the roster. He stated that he was going to pray for me while I slept and started praying. Needless to say, it was hard for me to sleep because this all to seemed both crazy and creepy at the same time.

I eventually went to sleep, only to be awakened by Collins telling me it was time to go to the onsite church service they had that morning. I told him that I didn't want to go to church because I was tired. He said, "God told me to tell you that he will not let you rest until you submit to him." Still skeptical and cynical, I told him, "I'm not sure what you're trying to do, but I want you to leave me alone."

He replied, "I am not bothering you, its God trying to get through to you." Because of his persistence, I agreed to go to church and planned to come back to my cell and take a nap.

We went to church, and Collins immediately started telling people that I was his friend and that God sent me there. Collins asked me to talk and say a few words to the people. I spoke for about 15 minutes, and the inmates were so touched by the message that they began to cry and praise God. I thought to myself, "I don't know why all of this is happening, and I asked God why I was here. I got back to my cell, and there was a line of inmates outside of my cell asking me to pray with them and to counsel them. I was amazed at the experience and was quite baffled at the turn of events.

I realized that this event was for me to sit down and assess what God was doing with me. He showed me that even during a storm, He could still use me. He put me in an unfamiliar place, looked beyond my flaws, and reminded me that purpose doesn't have an expiration date. That experience served as a turning point in my life and was God's way of showing me that it doesn't matter what happened in my life, once I truly surrendered to Him, He was going to use me for His glory.

The wind and those waves that God commands are often times what He uses to get our attention when He wants to take us in a different direction. And because His thoughts and ways are higher than ours, it can be quite uncomfortable for us to let Him navigate such a seemingly unstable situation. But remember that God is the captain of your ship, and He knows just when to kedge. He knows the right time and right place to drop the weight, and exactly where it should be placed. We just have to be willing to give Him control of that part of our lives. Honestly speaking, that can be very scary, because you have to be willing to give up control without completely knowing what's coming. You never know when God will kedge. And giving up control isn't the most natural thing for anyone to do, especially a person who prefers to be in control of things all the time. If you had things your way, you'd kedge at the first sign of wind roaring or waves crashing in. Not every wind and wave can kill you or cause damage, but you don't know that, so it makes you cautious and fearful more than it makes you confident that the Lord will see you through the very thing that He is commanding.

You have not truly walked in your faith until you have been persecuted or gone through great storms for your Godly beliefs and practices. Every person genuinely seeking God has to have a Judas encounter to solidify their strength. How can you imply that you want to be more like Jesus in faith, but have not had it tested and galvanized by haters? Haters come as a part of the elevation process. Remember that Jesus came so that you might have life and have it more abundantly. Therefore, as storms toss you back and forth, your stability of faith must be grounded in God's purpose for your life.

Let me ask you: Are you grounded? If not, why? Is it because your need for control won't allow you to trust God as the captain of your life's ship?

Stabilization Comes With Some Loss

When God is bringing you to the point of stability, it's going to feel as if you're losing a lot, especially when things become so unstable. There is a lot that will shift and be shaken up at the same time. You will suddenly start to feel like you're in between your best and worst days. You'll lose your grip on certain things when God is stabilizing you because your hands will probably free themselves up to grab hold of something that you don't want to lose. The interesting thing about that is, the very thing that you don't want to lose is what God wants you to get rid of. What's currently in your hand that you have a tight grip on? What's something that you don't want to let go of? It's probably a weight that He wants you to drop. This isn't to imply that what's in your hand is a bad thing; it just means that it's a weight. It's a weight He wants you to give to Him so that He can kedge. He uses the things that you don't need to anchor you and provide you with the mental and emotional stability you need during difficult times.

Being in ministry has heightened my awareness of the mental illness. Mental illness is so much more complicated than any pill that any mortal could invent. Mental illness is so much more than what the media and society have tried to make of it.

It goes much deeper than someone having something "wrong" with them. My heart goes out to those that struggle with those types of obstacles in life. As the church, we have a responsibility to address this issue and help those individuals who struggle with this issue feel embraced by God and His people. What people may be dealing with is not about you but about the need to feel loved and accepted.

Therefore, I no longer question what is wrong with people but instead, what has happened to them. Mental instability may come as a result of the mistakes and challenges people face in life. It is often said that people are the sum total of their life experiences. In other words, a person's character is an absolute result of what has transpired in their life. Experiences shape us. Experiences, both good and bad, mold our minds. They influence the way that we think about ourselves and life, they become the filter that we use for everything that happens.

It's often the lack of mental and emotional stability that causes us to make a lot of the mistakes that we make in life. When frustration or sudden changes take place, the first thing that rises to the surface is our emotions. If we haven't learned how to manage our emotions healthily, they'll drive us into decisions based off of a moment that could possibly create a conundrum. Emotions can be so fleeting at times that we allow a five-minute situation to become an entire day for us. You're mad one second and unbothered the next. You then think about that five-minute situation again, resulting in you being angry again.

You may let that 5 minutes roll into the next day, then the next, and eventually, you find yourself hung up on a situation for 5 months. Depending on the severity of the situation, you might be hung up on it for 5 years. Unfortunately, this is how many of us approach life; unstable and unhealthy both emotionally and mentally. Our emotions are the lord of our decisions and the captain of our ship. I would even go so far as to say that for many of us, our emotions are our preference. They are what we would rather respond with than rational, logical, and intelligent thinking. But if we are going to achieve stability, then we have first to be willing to let go of the preferences that we let govern our lives. We need to begin responding to life by allowing God to purify our desires so that we are riding the waves of life instead of erroneously navigating them without a captain that knows the way that we take.

Problems are often tools that develop us for a better walk with God.

Let's look at the parable in Luke chapter 13, verses 6-9. Here we find a man that had planted a fig tree, and for three years, it was barren. To the man that planted a fig tree, he had invested enough, and it was time for the tree to be destroyed. To the gardener, he saw an opportunity to prune, fertilize, and water before cutting the tree down. The gardener wanted another chance to try something different before accepting defeat. He was not willing to be defeated by stagnation, he saw it as a challenge to move in a different direction. How many of us are willing to move away from old ways of doing things, even in trouble, and rely completely on God? Problems are often tools that develop us for a better walk with God.

A Christian is nothing but a fallible human who puts himself or herself through school for Christ for the sole purpose of becoming better. The greatest of tragedies are often moving us towards the more magnificent walk of destiny.

> A Christian is nothing but a fallible human who puts himself or herself through school for Christ for the sole purpose of becoming better.

REFLECTION THOUGHT:

We have established that storms come, and they are beneficial for us when we allow our minds to believe that they are. You may be in the middle of a storm now, and it is seemingly overwhelming you mentally and emotionally. If that's the case, view the hardship through a positive filter, so you don't mismanage the storm or miss out on its excellent produce.

KEY SEVEN

Tune your Mind to Success

OBJECTIVE:

To equip you with the tools of change and impact, giving you a fresh sense of vision for discovering and living an extraordinary life.

"Don't let others define you. Don't let the past confine you. Take charge of your life with confidence and determination and there are no limits on what you can do or be."

– Michael Josephson

The Power of the Mind

Success is never by accident. One of my favorite authors is Bruna Martinuzzi, who teaches on developing practices of success. Her writings have helped shift my thinking and reduced my complacency. Warren Bennis says, "We seem to collect information because we can do so, but we are so busy collecting it that we haven't devised a means of using it. The true measure of any society is not what it knows but what it does with what it knows."[1] It is not enough to say you are educated,

Success is never by accident.

whatever knowledge you have gained needs to be carefully applied. Your knowledge is only worth something once it can be used in solving real-life issues. In today's world, there is a wealth of knowledge at our disposal. You can either drown in it or put it to good, practical use. Information without application is powerless. This chapter will discuss several valuable tips, based on discoveries in brain research, that can help you improve your personal and professional life as well as the lives of others around you.

Pay attention to the Pertinent Sources

A critical factor in our thought process is the ability to address the mental and medical aspects of things in our lives

---

1 How to Train Yourself To Be More Successful (Mindwalker. co.za)

that are considered relevant, which makes a tremendous contribution to your success and your perception of it. There is a close relationship between psychology and religion. There are many examples in the Bible of the mental aspects of who we are. Therefore, all of the things in our mind are relevant to who we are and how we see ourselves. This is what the Bible implicates when it states that "as a man thinks in his heart, so is he". This is why you have to be extra careful with where you get information and what type of information you allow into your heart.

Pertinent Negatives

In the medical realm, Pertinent Negative is a term that addresses a diagnosis of your past. It is an element of the patient's history that aids diagnosis because the patient denies that it is present. You have to be honest with yourself and address the things that may have negatively impacted your thought process or your ability to move forward in life. We often utilize denial as a defense mechanism and a way of masking the pain we have felt or may be feeling. However, we are running from not only ourselves but delaying the process of moving into a more magnificent walk of our future. You can't honestly face what you refuse to confront. To go forward, you have to give yourself permission, to be honest about the details of your past.

You can't honestly face what you refuse to confront.

129

Yes, it happened. Yes, it was traumatic, Now what? You must move on. Moving on starts with honest admission and acceptance of the negative experiences that have shaped you into the person that you currently are.

If you incur an injury and you go to the hospital, the first thing they ask you is, "Where is the pain, describe it." This gives the doctor more information to address and adequately treat your condition. Without this information, it would be difficult for them to formulate a plan of action that will aid in your betterment. Similarly, that is also how it works in real life. If you cannot be honest with yourself and God about the source of your pain and where you're hurting, then you will continuously apply remedies to superficial areas of yourself, ultimately finding yourself never discovering true healing.

QUESTION:

What truths do you need to address with God?
Lighten your load. God wants all of your burdens.

Pertinent Positives

On the other hand, we have Pertinent Positives, as well. In the medical terms, it is an element of a patient's history that aids diagnosis because the patient affirms that the pain is present. At that very point, this is where identifying the source of pain is activated. The ability to describe and admit the experiences makes the road to recovery easier and possible. I would suggest having the courage to stand up and look at your situation and experiences right in the eye. This will give you the ability to fight and overcome them. God gives us everything we need to activate the power within us. Are you operating in your greatest potential? What pertinent positives do you need to affirm?

Pertinent Traits

According to the Legal Information Institute, character evidence is admissible in a criminal trial if offered by a defendant as circumstantial evidence—through reputation or opinion evidence—to show an alleged victim's "pertinent" character trait—for example, supporting a defendant's claim of self-defense to a charge of homicide.[2]

It has been stated that the most significant indicators of your future are referencing your past. When the police are searching for a criminal, one of the first places they look is past places or activities because that is the typical psychological behavior of most humans. The Bible even references the dog returning to his vomit.

The current state of your life is the result of your pertinent habits, good or bad. We have a natural propensity to want to dwell in a place of comfort, but we must now use those indicators as a means of coming out of ordinary caves of our

2 Rule 404. Character Evidence; crimes or other acts - Cornell Law School

lives. The Bible teaches us that "before a man builds a house, he must first count the cost".[3] Building a house of success requires a price. The price for you to grow spiritually and emotionally should be losing the old you and developing a new you. When you were a child, you spoke as a child and acted as a child, but when you become a person of God, you put away childish things and adolescent thoughts.[4]

The question now becomes: what keeps people stuck in this cycle? The answer is you must deal with your undesired emotions.

Psychological Projection: Dealing With Undesirable Emotions

The Basics of Psychological Projection

The theory of psychological projection is also known as the 'Freudian projection' which was developed by Sigmund Freud. Sigmund Freud is also known as the "father of psychoanalysis." During a session, he noticed among his patients that they would accuse others of experiencing the same emotions they were demonstrating.[5] For some reason, this helped them deal with their emotions better. An example of the Freudian projection would be a woman who cheated on her husband and accused him of doing the

---

3 Luke 14:28
4 1 Corinthians 13:11
5 Psychological Projection: Dealing With Undesirable Emotions | EveryDayHealth.com

same. In some cases, someone would yell at others because he/she felt others did the same. There is a typical projection that people neglect. This is the interaction with a person you do not necessarily like. These psychological projections are not always dramatic; they can be very subtle.

Most times, we project our emotions as a form of defense. We use these defense mechanisms to cope with our emotions when we are uncomfortable expressing or processing through them. We use it as a form of protection because we don't want to get hurt. Physical and emotional injuries are read the same way by our brains. Emotional hurt could, sometimes, be more painful because it can be reoccurring, whereas physical pain is only present when we are aware of it.

Now, these psychological projections can be resolved. The first step to resolving projections is acknowledging that those emotions (anger, jealousy, or hurt) exist. It is natural to experience these emotions. They are not bad, it is how you project them onto others. The impact of projection is dependent on how you resolve them.

Eliminate Self Sabotaging Behavior

A principal once shared a story with me about one of his students. He stated that a particular student was sent to his office each week and was considered by the staff to be a troubled at risk child. The student intentionally created distractions in the classroom that prevented other students from learning. His teacher explained to the principal that every time the class received an assignment, learning became difficult because of his distracting behavior.

The students were often given assignments where they had to present or read out loud to keep them engaged in the classroom. In an effort to help the student, The principle started to have the student complete his work in his office. He would intentionally have him read out loud in an effort to help him improve his speaking skills. He soon realized that the student struggled with reading and was not comfortable in a speaking forum. It became apparent to the principal that the student would cause distractions so the students would not pick on him or realize that he could not read. He asked the student for confirmation and soon confirmed the principal's suspicions.

Much like many of us, the student caused distractions in order to avoid dealing with his own feelings of inadequacy and insecurities. Sometimes in life we cause distractions and blame others for our own shortcomings. We sometimes think if we can derail the relationship or conversation by focusing on someone else's shortcomings, then we don't have to deal with our very own. We don't deal with pain of being hurt by our past so we develop coping mechanisms to coexist with our pain. We must remain intentional about not becoming the very thing that hurt us. If you want to deal with the past of your father leaving, you won't accomplish this by duplicating his behavior. Always aim to become better than the issue you are facing. Oftentimes, we have the proclivity to want to take the credit for things that are good but blame others for what we lack. To be vulnerable does not make us weak but it makes us strong. Vulnerability positions us for meaningful connections and relationships.

2 Corinthians 4:2 says, " We must refuse to wear masks and play games. We don't maneuver and manipulate behind the scenes. And we don't twist God's Word to suit ourselves. Rather, we keep everything we do and say out in the open, the whole truth on display, so that those who want to can see and judge for themselves in the presence of God.

We sometimes have taken off the spiritual crowns that God has bestowed upon us and instead have put on spiritual masks. Much like a masquerade party, day by day people live their lives as the person they are pretending to be. We are so inclined to hide our true identity and shortcomings because we fear that people will judge us or we just simply aren't ready to face ourselves. Many people have vices, addictions or struggles but allude the act of dealing with these issues.

Much like the student, we would rather deal with the consequences of the avoidance than embrace the possibilities of victory. As a result, we are active participants in self sabotaging behavior by avoiding our internal issues and doing the necessary work required to become better people.

As a child we are born with 2 fears, we are born with the fear of failing and the fear of loud noises. In a figurative sense, we are afraid of failing and dealing with the fact that we may not always be successful. When in fact, the most successful people have often failed. The fear of loud noises in this context figuratively represents the noises we hear in our head. Sometimes, we can be our own biggest setback.

The power of the subconscious mind if we aren't careful can become louder than hearing the voice of God. If you subconsciously don't believe the power you possess through Christ, then you will always live in doubt and subconsciously do things contrary to his word.

Therefore, we must get out of our own way, and speak life over ourselves walk in dominion and relinquish the power we have within. Debbie Ford stated" The question "Is this an act of self-love or is it an act of self-sabotage?" is one you must consistently ask yourself if you are committed to having all that you want and all that you deserve. When you love yourself, you feel worthy and deserving of claiming the gifts of this world. Self-love gives you peace of mind and balance. Self-love gives you self-respect and the ability to respect others. It gives you the confidence to stand up and ask for what you want. Self-love is the main ingredient in a successful, fulfilled life.

You must be willing to do what others refuse to in order to obtain what others don't have.

Tune Out the Noise

The one thing we worry about that holds us back is our perceived opinions of what others say about us. The student was so worried about what the other kids would say about him that he was not willing to grow on his own. As adults, we are so concerned on what others will say about us that we don't take the time to address our internal struggles.

Paul tells us in 1 Corinthians 4:1-5 This, then, is how you ought to regard us: as servants of Christ and as those entrusted with the mysteries God has revealed. Now it is required that those who have been given a trust must prove faithful. I care very little if I am judged by you or by any human court; indeed, I do not even judge myself. My conscience is clear, but that does not make me innocent. It is the Lord who judges me. Therefore judge nothing before the appointed time; wait until the Lord comes. He will bring to light what is hidden in darkness and will expose the motives of the heart. At that time each will receive their praise from God.

In these verses, the Apostle expresses the truth that since he is the Lord's servant and steward, it is to the Lord that he owes responsibility and it is the Lord who judges him for the quality of his service. Human judgment has little value. Even self-evaluation is unreliable, Paul says. Christ is the Lord of the conscience and is the one who can evaluate it properly.[6] We have succumbed to others opinions but more importantly we are in judgment of ourselves for our mistakes and shortcomings. God is our ultimate judge. We must learn to silence the external and internal noises of judgment.

How To Deal with Difficult Emotions

1. The Giving Approach:

Why did people not like Jesus? Keep in mind that He spent all his life giving to others. You can see the very essence of someone's heart by giving to them. When you truly love someone, you will always find a way to give selflessly. You can provide them with love, kindness, money, support, time, generosity, or simply serve them. The thing is, we have mastered the art of taking, but none of us fully embrace giving. There is a transfer of power that happens when you learn the spiritual transformation of energy that comes with loving someone who doesn't know what love looks like. Most of us come from a place of feeling like collateral damage in an involuntary game at someone else's expense. I have found that people will give you their body before they give you their heart.

In an ideal world, it would be the opposite, but because people have been hurt so bad, they have a hard time giving love. Why? Because love produces vulnerability, and most

---

6 Mare, W. H. (1976). 1 Corinthians. In F. E. Gaebelein (Ed.), The Expositor's Bible Commentary: Romans through Galatians (Vol. 10, p. 211). Grand Rapids, MI: Zondervan Publishing

of us aren't willing to be vulnerable simply because we don't want to risk getting hurt by those around us. God's greatest commandment is love. However, God loves when you give to others less fortunate than you. Proverbs 19:17 says, "Whoever is kind to the poor lends to the LORD, and he will reward them for what they have done."

This is such a humbling experience that makes life so much more rewarding in the spiritual realm. Learn to bless people with random acts of kindness, whether it be in words or deeds. You can buy someone's meal, or coffee in line at Starbucks, or gift cards, etc. Serve others in love just as God has served us in his Son, Jesus Christ. 2 Corinthians 9:6-8 states for us to remember: Whoever sows sparingly will also reap sparingly, and whoever sows generously will also reap bountifully. Each of you should give what you have decided in your heart to give, not reluctantly or under compulsion, for God loves a cheerful giver.

2. The Growth Approach:

You must proactively seek ways to grow mentally, spiritually, and emotionally. You have to challenge yourself to be better in areas you may have long avoided. Jabez said in 1 Chronicles 4:9-10, the prayer is a simple one: "And Jabez called on the God of Israel saying, 'Oh, that You would bless me indeed, and enlarge my territory, that Your hand would be with me, and that You would keep me from evil, that I may not cause pain.' So God granted him what he requested." Jabez knew that he was bigger than where he was. He didn't allow his past hurts, circumstances, or setbacks to stop him from believing God for more. No matter what you've been through in your life, always remember that God wants us to grow and to be elevated in all aspects of our lives. When we become Christians, we enter into a relationship with God, Jesus, and the Holy Spirit that will cause us to grow. Through the power of the Holy Spirit, we are called to become more like Jesus and to become more holy. It is this spiritual growth that becomes a birthmark of our faith!

3. Going the Extra Mile Approach:

"And whoever compels you to go one mile, go with him two."
(Matthew 5:41)

The true essence of doing something different requires the actual execution and the dedicated move in the change. The choice to decide to do something different requires a concentrated and devoted effort to go further than you usually would. Ask yourself this question, how badly do you want the extraordinary life you know you were created to have? You must be willing to do what others refuse in order to obtain what others don't have. Be prepared to go the extra mile for what you want to achieve in life. If the door shuts in your face, take the stairs. Nothing is impossible if you stay committed to the journey.

There is a Power in Consistency

In the world today, we have so many options where we

can exercise the convenience of choices. We can quit on our commitments and have plenty of options that will sometimes take us off course if we don't apply wisdom. Webster Dictionary describes the consistency as steadfast adherence to the same principles, course, form, etc. There is consistency in a pattern of behavior. There is agreement, harmony, or compatibility among the parts of a complex entity. There is a level of commitment the Bible teaches us to have. We are to be consistent in the field to reap the harvest.

The consistency of prayer, studying, personal growth, marriage, and business require faithful practices. God teaches us in Galatians 6:9, "And let us not grow weary of doing good, for, in due season, we will reap, if we do not give up." The problem is, we sometimes quit before the process is complete. God wants us to remain faithful. To receive our harvest, we must plant, water, and nurture the seeds. We have to remain steadfast in our actions. Here are a few reasons why you should pursue consistency:

1. Consistency emphasizes faith over knowledge:

What gives someone the energy to do the same thing, again and again, every day? Some may say that as creatures of habit, we don't want to step outside of our comfort zone. There is some validity in that, but the other perspective is a thing of growth. God expects you to remain faithful to the vision and His purpose for your life.

The Bible talks of a double-minded man and how you cannot serve two masters. The ability to consistently pray and carry out the purpose requires a high level of courage and commitment. We have to commit to trusting God in spite of what we see but based on the things He has shown us.

We may not always know all of the facts of how it will look, but trusting God in the process is better than any knowledge someone could present to you. God may not always give you details, but he gives you a glimpse of your future. The Bible says that faith is the substance of things hoped for with evidence of things not seen. As we remain committed to his vision and promise for our lives, He will guide our path. Jesus said, "My sheep hear my voice, I know them, and they follow me . . ."7 An anointed person is not always faithful, but a faithful person will always be anointed to accomplish great things. When you are determined to remain faithful and committed to God despite the obstacles you face, he will reward you with more than you could have ever imagined. If you consistently and faithfully go to God, he will always reward you more than you could have ever imagined.

2. Consistency allows the planting of roots to grow and develop:

Growing up, I liked to play basketball. Sometimes, I would not want to go to practice, but I wanted to be good at the

7 John 10:27

game. My father told me that the way you practice is the way you will play. If you practice hard, you will be better during the game. That is how the art of undoing ordinary works. If you allocate your time and consistent commitment towards becoming good at whatever you want, then you will be more foundationally sound in your actions, practices, faith, journey, or anything you want. You have to integrate best practices that help you remain sharp and consistent in your approach.

3. Consistency works on all aspects of your life:

There are benefits to spiritual discipline. Discipline produces consistent behavior and reliability. For example, on your job, the employer relies on you and trusts that you will be on time and consistent in the quality of your work. Companies will reward a faithful person, in some instances, over the most qualified person. This applies spiritually as well. God does not always call the qualified, He qualifies the called. In the story of Moses, he made excuses and told God that he had a speech impediment. God told him that he was going to send Aaron with him so he could proceed with the mission. God gives each of us the tools we need to carry out the purpose of our lives. We must remain consistent and seek God so He can get the best out of our lives.

There is power in being faithful and consistent. The person that gives up never wins, and the person that wins never gives up. To be committed to change, you have to be focused.

You cannot be easily distracted or taken off course by outside forces.

REFLECTION QUESTION:

1. What are ways that you can change your perspective about what success truly is and how will influence your actions?
2. Are there certain insecurities you have that you project on others?
3. How can you develop healthy thinking habits and remain consistent in your spiritual growth journey?

Join the Company of "Un-Ordinary" Crazy People

OBJECTIVE:

To provide a launch pad and fuel for the amazing and many times crazy journey to extraordinary that is ahead of you.

Has following God ever made you look or feel crazy?

Un-ordinary people, to some degree, have to be considered crazy.

The ability to grasp change and fully embrace a new normal requires that you do un-ordinary things. There's no way around it. Having the audacity to believe that God can give you what you ask for requires a crazy faith, a bold faith. People will think you are out of your mind. King David, who the bibles describes, as a man after God's own heart, had to pretend to be crazy to preserve his own heart. Sometimes, life can be that crazy!

"David took these words to heart and was very much afraid of Achish king of Gath. So he pretended to be insane in their presence; and while he was in their hands he acted like a madman, making marks on the doors of the gate and letting saliva ran down his beard. Achish said to his servants, "Look at the man! He is insane! Why bring him to me? Am I so short of madmen that you have to bring this fellow here to carry on like this in front of me? Must this man come into my house?"
(1 Samuel 21:12)

This reminds me of a story I read about on NPR news of a mother in the northern part of Nigeria who pretended to be crazy to protect her daughter from Boko Haram terrorists.[1] The mother is famously known as Zainabu Hamayaji. In April 2014, the group abducted 276 female students and forced many of them to become their brides and renounce their faith. Can you imagine the horror these children must have felt, not to mention the pain they endured?

---

1 To save her children, she pretended to be crazy - NPR

According to the news, she heard that the group was approaching her community with the apparent intention of kidnapping young girls to prostitute, rape, and sodomize. She quickly and desperately came up with a plan to protect her 11-year-old daughter. She dug a hole behind her house and hid her precious daughter there with food and water, covered by a thin sheet of steel.

Each day, the men would come, and each time she would tell them she had no daughter, but they persisted, sensing that she was lying. And each time the men came, they would beat Zainabu up, demanding her to release her daughter to them. She has the scars to prove it, and then she decided to take things to the next level. She pretended to be mad, stripping herself and covering herself with filth. She would walk up and down the marketplace, mumbling like a crazy person.

After a while, the men decided that they did not want the daughter of a madwoman. NPR news writes that, though initially skeptical, the militants fell for her ploy. They also didn't kill her because they believed killing a mad person would have brought them bad luck. They also didn't want to marry a madwoman's daughter. This woman went through extreme lengths to save not only her daughter but also her family from the insurgents.

Faith is trusting God for what is humanly impossible.

Sometimes, we have to do the unthinkable to achieve the impossible. When we are faced with impossible situations, it takes crazy faith to trust God. The will to follow God requires that we trust him when we become hurt, go through pain and loss. We have to trust and have faith in God regardless of how things look in the present moment. I have had to wonder at times why would I continue to trust God if it keeps leading me to pain. The crazy part of it is, we find refuge in him even in times of despair. Despite what is happening around us, God's presence is the safest place. This makes trusting him easier.

Faith is trusting God for what is humanly impossible. Living an extraordinary life starts with believing God's promises. And they are many, and one of the things that should give you comfort is that God honors His word more than His name.[2]

The thing to realize is that the devil will attempt to take you out of character and cause you to doubt. He will go as far as to plant seeds of doubt and insecurity and even attempt to destroy your esteem and rob you of a peaceful place in your mind. The devil will try to take advantage of your weakness. The moment you put a stop to people and the devil, people define you as difficult selfish, or crazy because manipulators hate boundaries. They take from you and say you are the problem.

---

2 Psalm 138:2

As a follower of Christ, there will be times where you have to be crazy and fully understand that most people won't see what you see because God will show you things that people can't conceptualize.

In 1 Samuel 21, David went to Nob, to Ahimelek, the priest. Ahimelek trembled when he met him, and asked, "Why are you alone? Why is no one with you? David left from Nob after leaving his best friend Jonathan, headed to Gath. Nob was considered to be a Holy place of praise because it was next to Jerusalem and Judah. He left the place of praise headed to a place of pressing. He ended up in Gath in verse 10. In Greek, Gath means a place of wine pressing.

God takes us through a wine making process to make us extraordinary. When Paul said he presses toward the mark of the higher calling, he was saying he was willing to go through the pressing process. When he said, "the mark of the higher calling" he was talking about the goal of fulfilling the higher calling. In the pressing process, the goal is to produce wine.

Wine Pressing

A winepress is a device used to extract juice from crushed grapes during the wine making process. There are several different styles of presses that are used by winemakers, but their overall functionality is the same. Each style of press exerts controlled pressure to free the juice from the fruit (most often grapes).[3]

3 Winepress - Wikipedia.org

Pressure brings out what we have on the inside. It's like squeezing a tube of paste. You only get what's inside. We can pretend that we have it all together, smile in church, and raise our hands in worship, but it is the pressure that separates spiritual giants and grasshoppers. It is in the test that testimonies are born. God does allow pressure; this should not be confused as God punishing you or choosing to make you suffer.

We know that the devil comes to steal, kill and destroy, but when he makes you his target, rejoice, because it means God is about to do exceeding, abundantly more than you can ask or think. The pressure will propel you to your next level.

I believe we can learn some principles from how wine is made:

Step 1 – Harvesting:

The first step in making wine is harvesting. The process of making wine requires the gathering of the grapes to make the wine. The process is synonymous with the process of the mentally recorded episodes that make up who we are. Gathering experiences in life, situations, and circumstances to make you who you are. This is a process that allows us to gather all of the things that we have been exposed to. It develops the makeup of our minds.

Step 2 – Crushing:

After grapes are sorted, they are ready to be de-stemmed and crushed. Disappointments are the pain of things in the crushing process. The crushing season can be very painful, but this is how beautiful and valuable things are birthed. Gold has to go through the fire to be refined. God also promises comfort for the brokenhearted because it is only for a season; there is always light at the end of the tunnel. In his book, Crushing, Bishop T.D. Jakes aptly writes, "It's the nights that I cried myself to sleep, and my tears crawled across the bridge of my nose that God often used to develop me into the person I am today."[4]

Step 3 – Fermentation:

Fermentation is the process in which a substance breaks down into a simpler substance. Fermentation comes from the Latin word, 'ferment' meaning "to leaven." Leaven means to a persuasive influence that modifies something or transforms it for the better. Obtaining of the Holy Spirit and the anointing is the process of gaining the potency of making you great and positions you to live an extraordinary life.

Step 4 – Clarification:

Once fermentation is complete, clarification begins. Clarification is the process in which the unnecessary particles

---

4 T.D. Jakes, Crushing: God turns pressure into power

Undo Ordinary

fall off. The wine is then transferred or "racked" into a different vessel and can later be clarified through fining or filtration. The word, 'discern' means to distinguish and to separate out by diligent search. God gives us clarity through discernment. A discerning mind demonstrates wisdom and insight that go beyond what is seen and heard.

Step 5 – Aging and Bottling:

Aging and bottling is the final stage of the wine making process. A winemaker has two options: bottle the wine right away or give the wine additional aging. The longer the aging process, the finer and more expensive the wine. Wisdom is a virtue that isn't innate but can only be acquired over time and through experience. Anyone interested in trying new things and reflecting on the process can gain wisdom. By learning as much as you can, analyzing your experiences, and putting your knowledge to the test, you can become a wiser person.[5]

Grapes have seeds in them, and then the seeds are planted to grow more fruit. God has to get you to a place of pressing and being squeezed so you can bear more fruit. Keep in mind that David was headed to a cave as he ran from Saul. He thought the cave was a place of refuge, but it ended up being a place of pressing.

---

5 How to Gain Wisdom: 13 Steps (with Pictures) - WikiHow

152

We will find ourselves in crazy places and in crazy situations in the quest to become better humans. When we follow what we feel is the purpose of our lives, it will defy logic at times. Your path will not be the same as everyone else's. Therefore, your revealed walk or path is not going to make sense to someone else because God is not talking to them, but he's talking to you.

Plant Seeds of Life

The problem a lot of us face is that we let our past sins cripple our movement into the new dimension of living an extraordinary life. There are some steps can take that help you mentally, spiritually, and emotionally walk out of your past with dominion.

God is doing some amazing things in all of us. He wants us to be agreeable, sympathetic, loving, compassionate, humble. God does not want us to operate in retaliation or sharp-tongued sarcasm. Instead, He wants us to bless, encourage, and uplift the people around us. Be a blessing, so you will also be in the right position to receive a blessing. If you ever want to have a life worth living, "Say nothing evil or hurtful; snub evil and cultivate good; run after peace for all your worth."[6] When you listen and obey Him, you sow a seed of blessing. Seeds grow in silence but produce the most exceptional fruits.

---

6 1 Peter 3: 8-12, MSG

The thing that we must see here is that God has planted us as seeds on earth, as a representation of Him. All seeds that are planted require water, oxygen, and proper temperature to produce fruit or germinate. It is much like our spirit; we need those components to feed our spirit and tap into our inner power. We require water to live, but we require living water to survive. Water represents birthing in the Bible and life. When women have a baby, their water breaks, which means the birthing of life. Water is an essential symbol for Christians. Water is symbolic in the renewing of the soul in baptism. It may also signify a cleansing or purity.

Some seeds require proper light also. Some seeds need a lot of light to grow while others grow in darkness. Every seed has a specific condition that is conducive to its growth. Water and oxygen are taken in through the seed coat.[7] The coat of protection we have as Christians is the protection of the Holy Spirit.

All of us desire intimacy from others but we do desire intimacy more with the Heavenly Father? Having those emotions is how we know we abide in Him, and He in us. Our personal associations, material items or accomplishments does not give us status or royalty in the kingdom. God has assigned each of us to come in the spirit of service which then activates the aroma of intimacy and then triggers the virtue of love with the Messiah.

---

7 Great Plant Escape - Germination | Illinois.Edu

Fight for Your Future

A revolutionary in the spirit is willing to address things that others are not willing to fight with. There are several times the Bible addresses explicitly past spiritual vices. As a person that wants to undo the ordinary, there is a certain amount of boldness or eagerness to change "generational curses" that have plagued your family or life for quite some time. This boldness might seem crazy those around you, but always remember the generations to come will need you to move into another dimension in Christ.

Generational curses come in the form of cycles. Some people struggle with cycles of poverty, loss, or grief that may be traced back to their bloodline. For instance, a man may have struggled with alcohol, and if his son is not careful, he can struggle with the same thing. These cycles may not be noticed immediately and may have stemmed from a sin that took place decades ago. It is important to break every generational curse in your life if you ever want to live an extraordinary life. It's time to let go of everything that could be holding you back from living a life of purpose.

The Bible says we wrestle not against flesh and blood but against powers and principalities.[8] By law, the consequences of sin move down through the bloodline. If a father lived in sin, his children were bound to do the same. It may not seem fair, but it was believed that the children would repeat

---

8 Ephesians 6:12

the mistakes their fathers had made. However, this shouldn't make you think every single bad thing that happens to you is a result of a generational curse. The law to revisit the sins of fathers on future generations is an Old Testament law. We, now, live under grace through Jesus Christ.

If you experience curses attacking you from your lineage, I have come to tell you, there is a deliverance for it. The first step to this deliverance is acknowledgment and repentance. The children of Israel, in the Old Testament, were almost synonymous with a promiscuous wife. They would worship God today and worship idols the next day. They attracted curses because of the seeds they had sown. Sometimes, they would forget the faithfulness of their God and turn to made-made gods, but God was loving. If the Israelites repented, he would save them and break every curse. He also promised that He would extend his love to those that loved him and kept his commandments.[9] The same applies to us today. I want you to know that his grace is sufficient for you. His love is ever-present, ever sure.

You may ask, how can we deal with generational curses? It is through salvation – accepting Jesus as your personal Lord and Savior. For it is through salvation that we become new beings.[10] A child of God cannot have curses in their lineage if he/she consecrate themselves to a life of prayer and total

---

9 Exodus 20:6
10 2 Corinthians 5:17

commitment to God.[11]

A New Beginning

After reading this book, I am sure you would agree with me that you now possess the keys to a new beginning in your life. These keys give you access to the extraordinary life you were born to live. The number eight signifies new beginnings. I congratulate you on taking this opportunity to start afresh. Here are a few points to take with you as you begin this new chapter of your life:

1. Face the obstacles of life:

The first step to recovery is admitting or identifying the problems or struggles that you have or face. Sometimes, we play the blame game and choose to live in shame. Regardless of the obstacles we have faced, we are responsible for the choices and decisions we make. The challenge now becomes the reluctance to recognize them. You cannot address what you are not willing to face. So, remove the pain, remove the hurt, remove the memories. Make a decision to overcome it. You really don't realize how strong you are until you come face to face with some of your greatest challenges or weaknesses.

2. Remain Alert

When an engineer builds or design roads, the roads from are specifically designed to have hills, declines, twists, turns and

---

11 Romans 12:1-2

in most cases reflective markers. They have determined over time that including these items within the design will keep drivers aware and alert . Without them, drivers could become complacent, and perhaps find themselves less attentive while on their journey. Sometimes God allows obstacles, hills, declines and twists and turns in our life to keep us spiritually alert and to draw us closer to him. Without these obstacles, we wouldn't know the true meaning of perseverance, tenacity and unwavering faith. It is through life's unpredictable twists and turns that he reveals the true essence of who he is, and who we are in him.

3. Remove the rope of bondage

Spiritual chains can manifest in the form of habits, customs, and mindsets. They usually stem from old family traditions or difficult habits. It could range from abusive relationships to discrimination against a particular race. There is no bondage in Christ. There are ways you can untie every bondage in your life:

- Forgive yourself. Remember, "To err is human, to forgive is divine." Forgive yourself, then, forgive others.
- Invest in an accountability partner. Share with them your struggles and how you want to overcome them. A partner will keep you responsible and help you keep to your word. Be in good company. Stay around people who would help you grow.
- Engage in activities that bring you joy. Surround yourself

with people that love you. This will give you the strength to carry on with the day.

4. Put an end to the course of the curse:

Recognize that it is only the enemy who comes to steal, kill and destroy. Identify the issues in your life and get to the root of it. Forgive those who may have hurt you in the past, and commit to letting it go. It is the only way you can move on.

5. Love conquers:

We know, in our walk with Christ, that love conquers it all. It is in loving God, us, and others that we let go of the things that hold us emotionally and mentally captive. Love those who chastise you, persecute you and sin against you, your reward is great in heaven. There is a blessing that comes from unconditional love. On the other hand, accept God's love for you. There should be no room for hurt and sorrow. Do not accept condemnation. There is, therefore, now no condemnation to them which are in Christ Jesus . Perfect love casts out all fear. Corrie Ten Boom says, "There's no pit so deep that God's love is not deeper still."

6. Obedience is better than sacrifice:

One of the best ways to get to God's heart is through obedience. When you love someone, you do all you can to please that person. You need to be obedient to His will and surrender your will to Him. If you want to break free from curses, learn to obey the voice of God. You may not understand His instructions but do them anyway. There is a testimony lying at the end of every instruction.

7. Manage your emotions:

Are you looking at the glass half empty or half full? It is your attitude, emotions and perception of situations that affect your ability to have an extraordinary life. Are you sowing seeds of hurt or oppression? Are you sowing seeds of love and joy? The decision is in your hands. Your attitude should align with your identity in Christ. Your attitude and emotions can either bring favor or disfavor. Align yourself with God's word. Let your positive actions overshadow the negative ones.

Conclusion

Ordinary is a relative term depending on your perspective of reality. However, the challenge now becomes deciding whether or not you are really receptive to moving into a different dimension in your life, or are still holding onto some things that are really more detrimental to your spiritual growth. Life comes with its hurt, pain, and challenges, and these shape our perception of life and how we deal with people. We all struggle with discerning when to exercise patience or when to let some things or people go. In the spirit of wisdom, we are challenged with finding the right balance between patience and speed. We are afraid of releasing the past to embrace the future. This very thought process has immobilized many of us.

You can not be ordinary and stand out at the same time. The ability to recognize your greatness is one of the best gifts you can present to yourself. The boldness to change your mind, heart, and soul requires a tremendous amount of courage that we all innately possess. The difficult part is moving forward with courage and choosing something different other than what we have become accustomed to because change can be hard. This may come in the form of church, ministry, work, parenting, schooling, past hurt, pain. It may even be as simple as listening to a new perspective. You have to remain committed to change and take proactive steps towards becoming the change you want to see.

This book has provided tangible tools to help you move from a place of pain to a place of healing and deliverance. When you choose to undo the ordinary in your life, you will stand out. Sometimes, you may wonder if you made the right decisions. Don't give up, and stay committed to the process. Remember, the person without the Holy Spirit does not accept the things that come from the Spirit of God but considers them foolishness, and cannot understand them because they don't understand the principles of the Spirit.

The Spirit makes you deal in spiritual transactions that appear crazy to the spiritually immature. This will also require that you be crazy enough to challenge yourself to change. You have to be crazy enough to hold yourself accountable. You have to be crazy enough to break the curses of your family, tradition, habits, relationships, choices, and even sometimes, how you see God. We sometimes limit how we see God, which, in turn, limits how we see ourselves.

I hope this book helps you let go of the past. I hope these words will help you live a life of freedom, excitement and enthusiasm. I hope these tips help you hear God's voice clearly. I hope you feel led by the spirit to do crazy and exciting things for the kingdom. Most importantly, I hope these words help you deal with the obstacles to living a life filled with purpose. We have "an extraordinary God who produces extraordinary people." I urge you to use these keys very wisely. Undo the ordinary.

STEPS TO MY EXTRAORDINARY LIFE:

After reading Undo Ordinary, what are 3 practical action steps you sense you need to take right now?

_____

_____

_____

_____

Made in the USA
Columbia, SC
10 January 2023

75892111R00091